EXPLO

Martha's Vineyard

ON BIKE AND FOOT

LEE SINAI

Illustrations by Joyce S. Sherr

The Harvard Common Press
Boston

Contents

Introduction

Welcome to Martha's Vineyard, an island filled with unspoiled scenic areas! This book will lead you to those special places, guide you through them, and inform you about their history and unique natural features. *Exploring Martha's Vineyard on Bike and Foot* can also serve as a comprehensive guide to the Vineyard, since it describes the island's major attractions as well as its hidden treasures.

Martha's Vineyard contains six distinct towns and a wide variety of natural areas, but it is a surprisingly compact island, stretching just 23 miles from the Gay Head cliffs at its western tip to the Chappaquiddick beaches at the eastern end. Because the island is small and has fairly level terrain, it's an ideal place to bike or hike. With recent additions, the island will soon have 42 miles of bike paths that allow for relaxing exploration without worries about traffic, parking, or speed limits. Dozens of footpaths and hiking trails make the Vineyard a fine place for walking, too.

Exploring Martha's Vineyard on Bike and Foot contains 33 chapters. The first 14 chapters describe rides for bicyclists and the next 19 tell about the places you can explore on foot. Each of the bike rides in chapters 1–14 leads you to at least one destination—a beach, a town, a wildlife preserve, or a conservation area—where, if you like, you can continue on foot, using the appropriate chapter from chapters 15–33 as your guide. Each of the chapters in Part Two, "On Foot," includes directions from one of the island's major roads, for those who arrive by car.

The chapters are arranged geographically and follow the order

Destinations	Swimming	Picnicking	Scenic views	Entry fees	Off-road biking	Primitive roads	Botanical interest	Historical interest	Chapter number
State Forest		X			X		X		3
Katama Point and South Beach	X	X	X						4
Vineyard Haven and Herring Creek Beach	X	X	X			X		X	6
Edgartown and Lighthouse Beach	X	X	X					X	15
Sheriff's Meadow Sanctuary			X				X		16
Caroline Tuthill Wildlife Preserve			X				X		17
Felix Neck Wildlife Sanctuary			X	X		X	X		18
Brine's Pond Preserve		X			X		X		19
Chappy Five Corners Preserve		X			X		X		20
Mytoi		X	X			X	X		21
Poucha Pond Reservation		X	X		X		X		22
Wasque Reservation	X	X	X	X		X	X		23
Oak Bluffs Camp Ground		X						X	24
Tisbury Meadow, Wompesket, and Ripley's Field Preserves		X			X	X	X		25

trails. If you have a touring bike and are determined to reach a specific destination, you can walk your bike on these sandy or rocky sections. Each of the biking chapters and the chart on page ix indicate what type of terrain to expect and which properties permit biking on their trails.

Depending on the weather and your vehicle, you may prefer to drive to a destination and only hike. If you have young children who are not able to ride the distance or if you are headed for areas where parking is not a problem, this alternative is a good one. Another possibility is to put your bikes on or in your car and drive part of the way, park your car, and then bike. The entrances to the bike paths at the State Forest, marked on the biking maps with a P, are good places to leave your car. Other parking areas are marked by P's and are also listed in the appendix.

Many of the walking chapters describe several trails. You can choose to walk on one, two, or all of them. Before you hike, read through the text to decide which trails appeal to you.

BIKING EQUIPMENT

If you are taking one of the bike rides described in chapters 1–13, make sure you have the necessary gear before setting out on your trip. Check your bike carefully to prevent your being stranded because of faulty brakes or a flat tire. In the appendix (page 183) you will find a list of emergency phone numbers and addresses, including the phone numbers of bicycle shops and service stations should your tires need air.

The following is a checklist of necessary items for your bike trip:

1. Full water bottle
2. Helmet
3. High energy snacks
4. Tool kit
5. Tissues
6. Suntan lotion
7. Sunglasses
8. Small first-aid kit
9. Insect repellent
10. Bike lock
11. Towel, if you will be swimming
12. Comfortable walking shoes, if you will be hiking

Poison ivy

POISON IVY AND TICKS

Even a spot as wonderful as the Vineyard is not without its
hazards. **Poison ivy** and ticks exist on the island, but they
should not present a problem if you take the proper precautions.
I have spent the last ten years hiking in the woods and I have
not had poison ivy nor have I had a tick attach itself to me. But I
am careful.

To avoid poison ivy, which grows all over the island, you
have to know what it looks like. It has clusters of three green
leaves which are shiny if the plant grows in a sunny spot and
dull if it is in the shade. In the autumn, its leaves are bright red
and its white berries may be mistaken for bayberry fruit. The ivy
can grow like a vine, climbing up a tree, or it can spread along
the ground among bushes or on sand dunes. If your skin comes
into contact with poison ivy, wash the affected areas with strong
soap as soon as possible.

Ticks live on tall beach grass and in brushy areas. You often
can see them hanging on to the tips of grasses or leaves waiting
to grab onto a warm-blooded traveler. These arachnids come in
two varieties, the pinhead-size deer tick and the quarter-inch
dog tick. They usually attach to the legs and then move upward.

from Memorial Day to Columbus Day. Each lands in Oak Bluffs and none carries cars.

The Woods Hole, Martha's Vineyard, and Nantucket Steamship Authority boats (508-540-2022) are larger, carry cars, and run year-round. The trip takes 45 minutes and lands in either Vineyard Haven or Oak Bluffs. In Falmouth, there is a parking lot close to the ferry. However, parking in Woods Hole can be a problem: the lot near the ferry is often full and cars are routed to other lots. Passengers then must ride a shuttle bus or bike from the parking lot to the ferry dock. The 3.25 mile Shining Sea Bikeway, located 0.25 miles to the right of the main parking lot on Palmer Avenue, leads to the Steamship Authority Dock in Woods Hole.

If you arrive on the Vineyard by plane, you can grab a cab or shuttle bus from the airport to your lodgings and rent a bike at one of the many bike rental shops listed in the appendix.

ISLAND FACILITIES

Martha's Vineyard provides shuttle buses from May through October. For a nominal fee they will transport you between the major towns. The buses run every half hour in the summer and every hour during the spring and fall.

Two commercial campgrounds are located in the center of the island. The Martha's Vineyard Family Campground (508-693-3772) is situated one half mile from Vineyard Haven center on the Edgartown-Vineyard Haven Road. Webb's Camping Area (508-693-0233) is on Barnes Road in Oak Bluffs.

The Manter Youth Hostel (508-693-2665) abuts the Manuel Correllus State Forest in West Tisbury.

UP-ISLAND, DOWN-ISLAND, WET, AND DRY

Visitors are often confused by island terminology. If a place is referred to as "down-island," the location is the eastern end of the island in the towns of Edgartown, Vineyard Haven, or Oak Bluffs. Of those towns, Edgartown and Oak Bluffs are "wet," of Watertown, Massachusetts, purchased Martha's Vineyard, Nantucket, and the Elizabeth Islands from two English noblemen. His son, Thomas Mayhew, Jr., along with other Englishmen, came to the Vineyard soon after the purchase and settled in Great Harbor, in what is now Edgartown.

These early English settlers, consisting of about eighty people, learned fishing, farming, and whaling from the friendly Wampanoags. The English, in turn, shared their Christian beliefs, particularly Reverend Thomas Mayhew, Jr., who successfully converted many Wampanoags to Christianity. When the Reverend did not return from a transatlantic voyage, his father, Thomas Mayhew, Sr., governor of the island, continued his son's missionary work. Three succeeding generations of Mayhews also were influential island preachers.

The sea and land provided sustenance for the English as it had for the Indians. Each of the six Vineyard towns developed its own character based on how its eighteenth century occupants earned a living. Even today, each town maintains an individuality that reflects its origins.

Vineyard Haven, which is incorporated as the town of Tisbury, was a popular port for the vessels that sold the Vineyard's whale oil, candles, salt cod, and wool to customers in Europe and the West Indies. Its residents earned their livings from the sea as sailors, pilots, navigators, and fishermen. Today Vineyard Haven's well-located harbor continues to be the island's main port of entry, welcoming the Martha's Vineyard Steamship Authority Ferry all year-round. As a result, it is the only town whose stores and restaurants remain open during the winter.

Oak Bluffs owes its origins to the resurgence of religion that sparked the annual summer gatherings at the Martha's Vineyard Camp Meeting Ground. The festive nature of these meetings created a resort-like atmosphere that pervaded all aspects of Oak Bluffs' development—from the ornate and colorful gingerbread cottages to the tourist-friendly shops.

The development of **Edgartown** was heavily influenced by the lucrative whaling industry. Homes, churches, and public buildings were built with whaling profits and the community

MAP SYMBOLS

.... Bike Route

Beginning of bike route

Beginning of foot trail

2 Chapter Numbers

② Noteworthy Sights

·······> Secondary arrow--used when routes overlap

Scenic Lookout

Lighthouse

Chappy Ferry

Automobile Parking

Hospital

Youth Hostel

Airport

Drinking Water

Martha's Vineyard Regional High School

Forest Supervisor's Residence

Osprey Pole

Takemmy Farm

Red Barn Emporium

Thimble Farm

Chicama Vineyard

S Solviva

Wetland Symbol

Salt Marsh

Part One

ON BIKE

1. Vineyard Haven to Edgartown Loop

This loop, an attractive ride in itself, also will take you to five of the walks described (Chapters 15–18, and 24) in Part Two of this book, as well as to the starting points for the off-road biking loop through the State Forest (Chapter 3) and for the Chappaquiddick bike ride (Chapter 5). The route begins on the inland Edgartown–Vineyard Haven Road and returns through Oak Bluffs via scenic Beach Road and East Chop.

Round-trip biking distance via the loop from Vineyard Haven:
To Edgartown: 17 miles
To Sheriff's Meadow Sanctuary: 18 miles
To Caroline Tuthill Wildlife Preserve: 16 miles
To Felix Neck Wildlife Sanctuary: 16 miles
To State Forest: 16 miles
To Oak Bluffs Camp Ground: 16 miles

Terrain: Several short inclines

Food and drink: VINEYARD HAVEN: Black Dog Bakery; A&P Supermarket; Norton's Farm; Portside Restaurant; Chowder House.
EDGARTOWN: Healthy Gourmet Natural Food Market.
OAK BLUFFS: Nancy's Snack Bar.

Restrooms: VINEYARD HAVEN: (1) On the left side of Union Street, as you disembark from the Steamship Authority Ferry. (2) At the rear of the A&P parking lot on Water Street.
OAK BLUFFS: On the left, as you face the Steamship Authority

3

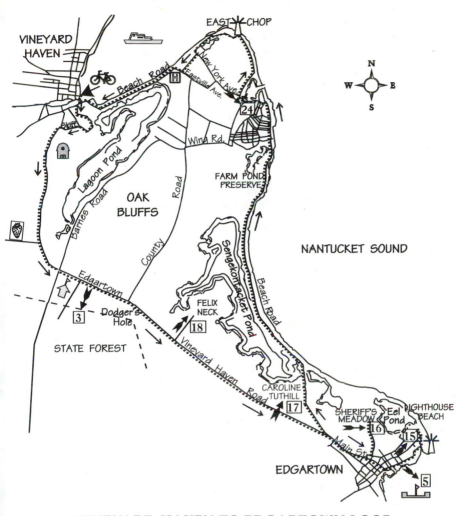

VINEYARD HAVEN TO EDGARTOWN LOOP

mile trail that passes through woodlands and by salt marsh, and skirts the shore of Sengekontacket Pond. See Chapter 17, page 103, for a guide to exploring the preserve on foot.

10 A half mile past the Tuthill Preserve is the intersection with Beach Road and the Triangle shopping area. On the right is Post Office Square, home of the Healthy Gourmet Natural Food Market, which sells a wide variety of nutritious foods and drinks.

11 To reach Cannonball Park, from which the **Edgartown** (Chapter 15) and **Sheriff's Meadow Sanctuary** (Chapter 16) walks and the **Chappaquiddick** bike ride (Chapter 5) depart, continue straight onto what is now called Upper Main Street. Cannonball Park, also known as Memorial Park, is at the next intersection.

12 To continue the loop back to Vineyard Haven, via Oak Bluffs, hook a sharp left onto Beach Road at the Triangle shopping area.

13 Beach Road, one of the most scenic on the island, travels by the two-mile-long **Joseph A. Sylvia State Beach**, on your right, and Sengekontacket Pond, on your left.

If you would like to stop and swim, park your bike in the rack in the small parking lot on the right side of the road. The beach tends to be wider and sandier at this end. Watch out for poison ivy as you walk to the beach.

14 After your swim, continue on Beach Road for another four miles, until you reach the heart of Oak Bluffs, passing Ocean Park on your left and the Steamship Authority Wharf on your right.

15 Continue straight, with the ocean on your right. When you reach a large parking area, where the Island Queen ferry picks up its passengers, hook a left.

22 At the "T" intersection, turn right, onto Eastville Avenue.

23 Eastville Avenue heads toward the water. At the intersection, turn left, toward Vineyard Haven.

24 You are now on another Beach Road—not the same as the one in directions #12–14 above. *This* Beach Road crosses a drawbridge over Vineyard Haven Harbor (to the right) and Lagoon Pond (to the left). The small, sandy spit that juts out into Vineyard Haven Harbor to your right just before the drawbridge is Eastville Point Beach, another place where you can stop and swim.

> If you are fortunate, you won't have to wait as the bridge opens and closes, which it does when boats travel between the pond and harbor. When a hurricane or northeaster is forecast, boats line up in the harbor to pass under the bridge, so that they can wait out the storm in protected Lagoon Pond.

25 This section of Beach Road is often busy. (Although it is not yet built as this book goes to press, the bike path designated for this stretch should be in place soon, allowing you to ride separately from the motor vehicles.) The Portside Restaurant, which rests at the edge of Lagoon Pond, on the left side of the street, is a good place to stop for a snack. Here you can sit outside and watch the windsurfers sailing by. Further ahead, also on the left in the Tisbury Market Place, is the Chowder House, which also has outdoor tables.

26 Shortly after the Tisbury Market Place is the "Five Corners" intersection. Walk your bike across the intersection and onto Water Street, which leads to Union Street and the Steamship Authority Wharf.

2. Oak Bluffs to Edgartown Loop

If you love the ocean, this bike trip is for you. The route from Oak Bluffs to Edgartown along Beach Road is one of the most scenic stretches on the Vineyard. Because the road hugs the three-mile length of Joseph A. Sylvia State Beach, a hot and tired cyclist can jump into the water at any time during the ride. Within this loop are six areas to explore, listed below with round-trip distances from Oak Bluffs. Each of the areas is described in later chapters. You can also access the Chappaquiddick bike ride (see Chapter 5) from this loop.

Round-trip biking distance via the loop from Oak Bluffs:
  To Edgartown: 15 miles
  To Sheriff's Meadow Sanctuary: 16 miles
  To Caroline Tuthill Wildlife Preserve: 14 miles
  To Felix Neck Wildlife Sanctuary: 14 miles
  To State Forest: 14 miles
  To Oak Bluffs Camp Ground: 14 miles

Terrain: Flat

Food and drink: EDGARTOWN: In the Triangle shopping area, Upper Main Street—Healthy Gourmet Natural Food Market; A&P Supermarket; Fresh Pasta Shoppe. In Edgartown Center— Among the Flowers Cafe; Wharf Pub; Mad Martha's; Mrs. Miller's Muffins.

Just ahead is the beginning of the **Joseph A. Sylvia State Beach**. Early morning swimmers frequent this beach for their daily exercise. Windsurfers, too, favor this beach because of its calm seas and steady winds. Later in the afternoon, when the wind picks up, the more adventurous windsurfers jump on their boards.

Less adventurous windsurfers can attempt the sport on the other side of the road, in the less intimidating **Sengekontacket Pond**. If the tide is low, windsurfers may be joined by clammers, since the pond supports an abundance of shellfish. In the autumn, Sengekontacket is a popular scalloping spot. If you decide to stop and swim, you can park your cycle in a bike rack at the far end of the beach, in a small parking lot on the left side of the road.

During late spring and early summer, a common island shrub, *Rosa rugosa*, flaunts its delicate pink blossoms. This sun-loving plant thrives on sandy soil and is commonly found alongside roads and beaches. In the fall, the blossoms become shiny, red, round hips, which are a great source of vitamin C.

The beach ends at a little stream called Menada Creek. Late in the day, young and old, armed with nets, wade in the creek and search for blue-claw crab for dinner.

3 Four and a half miles from Oak Bluffs Harbor, you will reach the intersection of Beach Road and Edgartown–Vineyard Haven Road. The intersection forms a wedge, called the Triangle, occupied by a number of shops and a few restaurants.

To reach Cannonball Park, from which the **Edgartown** (Chapter 15) and **Sheriff's Meadow Sanctuary** (Chapter 16) walks and the **Chappaquiddick** bike ride (Chapter 5) depart, continue straight onto what is now called Upper Main Street. Cannonball Park is wedged in the triangular convergence of Main Street, Cooke Street, and the Edgartown–West Tisbury Road.

The A&P Supermarket, which has a great bakery and salad bar and also sells ready-made sandwiches, is ahead on the eventually leaving a very large hole when it melted. Because the hole was deep enough to lie below the level of the water table, it formed a pond. However, Dodger's Hole is rapidly drying up and is now more bog than pond.

8 Pass County Road, on your right. Almost a mile ahead, on the left, is the Martha's Vineyard Regional High School. The access road to the **Manuel F. Correllus State Forest** lies between the school building and the playing fields. An off-road bike ride, described in Chapter 3, page 17, begins a mile down that road.

9 To continue on this loop, take your next right onto Barnes Road, a hilly but scenic ride. As you ascend and descend, views of Lagoon Pond appear on your right.

10 After pedaling for 2.5 miles, you'll reach the intersection with County Road. Turn left.

11 County Road ends at Eastville Avenue. Turn left.

12 Take the first right, onto Temahigan Avenue.

13 Remain on Temahigan until you reach Highland Drive, also known as East Chop Drive, which intersects on the left. Turn left.

On Martha's Vineyard there are two "Chops"—East and West. Here "chop" refers to the opening or entrance to a channel or body of water. Both of the Chops rise high above Vineyard Sound, guarding the entrances to the Oak Bluffs and Vineyard Haven harbors.

As you bike along East Chop Drive, look to your right for Crystal Lake, formerly known as Ice House Pond. Before the advent of refrigeration, local residents used the ice from this pond to keep their food from spoiling.

14 Continue on the drive to the lighthouse, perched high on the bluff, where you can dismount and enjoy the panorama.

3. Through the Manuel F. Correllus State Forest

The 4,343-acre Manuel F. Correllus State Forest is an ideal destination for off-road cyclists. It is crisscrossed with bike paths and it has fire lanes, horse trails, and remnants of "ancient" roads. My favorite loop includes each of these as well as a section of the Dr. Fisher Road, a narrow cart path created more than one hundred and fifty years ago by a wealthy Edgartown resident in order to carry grain to Edgartown from his grist mill in West Tisbury.

ABOUT THE STATE FOREST

In 1908 the Commonwealth of Massachusetts paid one dollar plus the back taxes for 612 acres of centrally located island land to use as a sanctuary for the endangered heath hen. However, the heath hen did not fare any better on the Vineyard than it did anywhere else. None has been seen in the forest for more than sixty years.

In 1925, the state began to take over much of the surrounding land. Within two years the forest had grown to its present 4,343 acres.

Due to frequent fires, which retarded tree growth, the forest remained a sandplain grassland habitat until 1934. In that year the Civilian Conservation Corps began to plant **red pine** trees, which the CCC thought would grow well in the sandy soil that had been left behind fifteen thousand years ago when the glacier retreated. Unfortunately, many red pines, which thrive in colder northern regions, adjusted poorly to the Vineyard's more

Edgartown bikers: Leave Edgartown on the
Edgartown–Vineyard Haven Road. Bike for 3.5 miles, until you
reach the Martha's Vineyard Regional High School, on the left.
Turn onto the road that lies between the high school and the
playing field. Pick up the directions below.

BIKING DIRECTIONS

1 After pedaling for a mile on the road between the high
school and playing fields, turn left at the barrier that prevents
cars from passing through. Pedal for a short distance on the dirt
road, past the wide, sandy fire lane. A lone pine tree sits in the
middle of the road.

2 Take the path to the right of the tree. This path, which is
also used as a horse trail, travels south over rough terrain for
about a mile.

3 Upon reaching the paved bike path, turn left, and pedal for
another 1.3 miles on this shaded, rolling stretch.

4 At the end of the bike path, turn left onto the sandy,
unpaved fire lane. To the right of the fire lane is a narrow and
less sandy bike path. Remain on this section for 0.6 miles.

If you are traveling in midsummer, look on the left side of
the fire lane for the many lowbush blueberry bushes.
Interspersed among the blueberries are clumps of the small
yellow flowers of wild indigo plants. This plant's name is
derived from the blue dye that is produced when the plant's
leaves are soaked in water.

5 Look closely on the left for the hidden trail that emerges
between the first and second telephone poles. Head onto this
path, a remnant of the old Dr. Fisher Road, which in the
nineteenth century was a main thoroughfare between North
Tisbury and Edgartown. This challenging mile-and-a-quarter
stretch is often overgrown. However, with the increasing
numbers of off-road bikers, this path may improve. If it looks as

The forest's Nature Trail, which you can explore on bike or foot, begins halfway down the hill on the left side of the road. Banks of red and white pine trees line the path. The trees can be distinguished by their needles. Red pines have two needles in each cluster; white pine clusters contain five needles. You may spot a pitch pine, the only pine tree native to the island. It has three needles in each cluster.

In 1991 Hurricane Bob caused immense damage in the forest, requiring considerable cleanup on the Nature Trail. As of this writing, many signs are down and the trail has not been completely repaired. However, the repair work should be completed soon.

As you leave the Nature Trail, look for Little Pond on your right. This depression, called a kettle hole, was created by the slow melting of a large chunk of ice that broke off from the retreating glaciers. It may or may not hold water, depending on the amount of rain that has fallen.

8 Continue down the hill, past the parking area, until you reach Barnes Road. Turn right.

9 Travel just under a mile. This will return you to the "blinker" intersection with the Edgartown–Vineyard Haven Road.

4. To Katama Point and South Beach

from Vineyard Haven

The route from Vineyard Haven to Katama Point and South Beach offers the security of bike paths for much of the way. At Katama Point you can swim in the calm waters of Katama Bay. At South Beach you can jump the waves and bodysurf.

Round-trip biking distance from Vineyard Haven: 22 miles

Terrain: A few short inclines

Food and drink: VINEYARD HAVEN: A&P Supermarket; Black Dog Bakery; Mad Martha's; Norton Farm.
EDGARTOWN: Katama Farms; Morning Glory Farm.

Restrooms: VINEYARD HAVEN: (1) Across from the ferry terminal building. (2) At the rear of the A&P Supermarket parking lot on Water Street.
EDGARTOWN: In the Visitors' Center on Church Street, between Main Street and Pease's Point Way.

Oak Bluffs bikers: Follow the directions in Chapter 2 to the Triangle intersection in Edgartown. Then pick up the directions below at direction #7.

BIKING DIRECTIONS

1 Begin at the Steamship Authority Wharf on Union Street. Proceed up Union Street and take the first left, onto Water Street.

7 The Edgartown–Vineyard Haven Road intersects with Beach Road, forming a wedge of land, called the Triangle, that is filled with shops and restaurants. At the intersection of the two roads, the name of the road changes to Upper Main Street. Continue on Upper Main, past the commercial establishments, until the road forks and you reach a stop sign for cyclists. Across the street sits Cannonball Park, the departure point for the rides that begin in Edgartown.

8 Fork right onto Cooke Street, following the signs to Katama and South Beach.

9 Take the first right, onto the Edgartown–West Tisbury Road.

10 Turn left onto Robinson Road.

11 Bike past the parking lot and bus stop.

In order to reduce automobile traffic, Edgartown runs a free shuttle bus into the business district. The town also operates a trolley to South Beach. Behind the parking lot lies the Edgartown recreation area, with playing fields and tennis courts.

12 Turn right at the next intersection, toward Katama, on Katama Road.

13 Pedal 0.3 miles on a narrow, congested stretch, until you reach the bike path on the left side of the road.

14 After biking a few minutes on the path, look to your right at the **Norton Fields Preserve**.

This 17-acre working farm is a property of the Martha's Vineyard Land Bank Commission, an organization that uses money from island real-estate transactions to acquire parcels of land. The Land Bank purchased Norton Fields in order to

Osprey

18 Return to Edgartown Bay Road, and turn left. Continue the loop, until you reach the entrance to **South Beach**.

South Beach, which stretches from Chappaquiddick to Edgartown Great Pond, allows extensive beach hiking along a continually changing landscape. The ocean here is advancing at an annual rate of eight feet, making the beach narrower each year. In some sections all that is left are the dunes.

For solitude, head for the eastern section of the beach. This section, which stretches toward Chappaquiddick, faces the ocean on one side and Katama Bay on the other. You can walk on either side, but if you cross from one to the other be careful to avoid walking on the fragile sand dunes. Dunes help to slow beach erosion, and the higher they are, the less the ocean can encroach on the land. Terns, which look like thin sea gulls, and **sandpipers**, small birds with long bills, inhabit this part of the beach.

If you want to swim, head for the mile-long lifeguard-supervised section of beach. The waves are strong here and there is usually a strong undertow. Rip tides, strong currents that flow rapidly away from shore, have occasionally caught unsuspecting swimmers. If you are caught in a rip tide, swim

23 Turn left onto the Edgartown–West Tisbury Road. The bike path that runs on the right side, along the edge of the forest, begins a mile ahead. (A bike path along the first mile should be completed soon.)

24 Remain on the path for three miles, until you reach Barnes Road. Turn right onto Barnes Road. The bike path is on the left side of this road and is largely hidden from view.

25 Pedal for two miles until you stop at the "blinker," the only traffic light on Martha's Vineyard. Turn left, toward Vineyard Haven, on the Edgartown–Vineyard Haven Road. You now will cover two miles of terrain that you biked earlier in the trip.

26 After the bike path ends, cross to the right side of the road and watch for Skiff Avenue. Turn right onto Skiff, to avoid the congested junction with State Road.

27 This is a great end-of-day run: a steep downhill enhanced by a view of Lagoon Pond. Turn left, at the end of the descent, onto Lagoon Pond Road.

28 Lagoon Pond Road joins four other roads at the hazardous "Five Corners" intersection. Walk your bike across the road, then continue on Water Street.

29 Water meets Union Street. A right turn here will take you to the ferry dock. A left onto Union Street will take you toward Mad Martha's, where you can reward yourself with an ice cream cone.

5. Chappaquiddick Loop

from Edgartown

Chappaquiddick, with its flat terrain and light traffic, is perfect for biking. Since there is only one major road, it's impossible to get lost. Off-road biking is permitted in Brine's Pond Preserve, Chappy Five Corners Preserve, and Poucha Pond Reservation.

Biking distance from Cannonball Park in Edgartown to:
  Brine's Pond Preserve: 1.7 miles
  Chappy Five Corners Preserve: 3.3 miles
  Mytoi: 2.8 miles
  East Beach: 3.5 miles
  Poucha Pond Reservation: 3.8 miles
  Wasque Reservation: 5 miles

Terrain:
  To Mytoi: 0.3 miles of unpaved road
  To East Beach: 0.8 miles of unpaved road
  To Wasque: 1.2 miles of unpaved, sandy road

Food and drink: EDGARTOWN: Midway Market; Soigné; Morning Glory Farm.

  CHAPPAQUIDDICK: Once you've crossed over to Chappaquiddick, the only place to purchase anything is the Chappy General Store, located on the left, 2.2 miles from the ferry. You can refill your water bottle at the hand pump at Wasque Reservation.

expectantly to the right side, the attendant will wave you on. Be prepared to pay the $2.50 round-trip cost during the crossing; no money will be collected when you return. After the two-minute ferry ride, the attendant will tell you when to disembark.

Before you proceed, look back toward Edgartown for a panoramic view of the town, with the lighthouse guarding the inner and outer harbors.

The first large complex of buildings on your left is the Chappaquiddick Beach Club, a private facility for families that summer on the island.

7 After biking for about a mile and a half, on your right you will see a tree-covered island sitting in a small pond. This area is **Brine's Pond Preserve**. Biking is allowed on the preserve's trails.

If you would like to explore Brine's Pond Preserve on foot, see Chapter 19, page 117.

The Chappy General Store, which carries a little of everything, is located on the left side, a half mile beyond Brine's Pond.

8 A half mile past the Chappy General Store, the paved road swings sharply right. To reach **Mytoi** and East Beach, continue straight onto the dirt road, following the sign to Mytoi. Mytoi lies 0.3 miles down the road. East Beach is a half mile further.

If you would like to explore Mytoi on foot, see Chapter 21, page 122.

9 To reach the remaining destinations, stay on the paved road until you reach the junction with Wasque Road. **Chappy Five Corners Preserve**, nestled in the right corner, permits bikers to negotiate its trails.

If you would like to explore Chappy Five Corners Preserve on foot, see Chapter 20, page 119.

10 Turn left at this corner to find **Poucha Pond Reservation**, located on the left next to Wasque Farm and immediately after

15 Turn right onto North Water.

The houses on the left side of North Water Street were built at an angle so their occupants would have a better view of the boats sailing into the harbor. After you pass Morse Street, look up onto the roof of the second house on the left. The balustrade on the top, called a "widow's walk," enabled the wives of captains of whaling vessels to look far out into the ocean as they anxiously awaited their husbands' return. Perhaps you'll spot Capain Jared Fisher's widow, who has been waiting for more than a hundred years.

Just before the road bends, look to your right at the **Edgartown Lighthouse**. The original lighthouse was built in 1828 on a small manmade island a quarter mile out into the harbor. One could only access it by boat; however, the next year a footbridge was built. In 1938 the structure was replaced, but by then it no longer sat on an island, since ocean currents had created a sandbar between the lighthouse and the mainland. A mile-long public beach extends from the lighthouse to Eel Pond.

16 Continue until you reach Fuller Street. Turn left. Don't miss the remarkable gardens that decorate the side yards of these fine old homes.

17 Fuller ends at Morse Street. Turn right.

18 Take your second left, onto Pease's Point Way.

19 Follow Pease's Point Way as it bends around and intersects with Main Street.

20 Turn right onto Main Street, which leads to Cannonball Park.

harbor was second only to the English Channel in the number of ships that passed through during journeys to and from Europe, Africa, and the West Indies.

The town thrived, catering to the thousands of vessels that harbored in its port. Many residents became pilots and accompanied ships on their journeys. Others provided sails, navigation equipment, food, and clothing. However, the opening of the Cape Cod Canal in 1914, combined with the increased use of trains, trucks, and steamships to move cargo, reduced the number of vessels passing through Vineyard Sound. Vineyard Haven continues to be the island's center for commercial sea traffic, but now its ferries carry the cargo that drives the island's main industry: tourism.

Biking distance: 7.5 miles

Terrain: Flat; 1 mile of unpaved road

Food and drink: VINEYARD HAVEN: Many fast-food establishments and restaurants line Main Street.

Restrooms: VINEYARD HAVEN: From the junction of Main and Spring Streets, take the first right into the parking lot. The restrooms are in the building on the left, next to the police station.

BIKING DIRECTIONS

1 Begin at the corner of Spring and William Streets. Facing downhill, turn right at William Street.

In the middle of the block, on the right and across from Camp Street, sits the handsome **Captain Richard C. Luce House** (number 1 on the map), built in 1883 for Luce, one of the Vineyard's most successful whaling captains. This Greek Revival–style home was the first of its size to be built in Vineyard Haven. Soon other whaling captains followed Luce's lead and built homes on William Street.

3 Proceed north up William Street, a designated historic district, past other Greek Revival-style captains' homes.

This street was spared during the 1883 fire that swept down Main Street and destroyed the town center.

4 *Don't miss* the right turn onto tiny Colonial Street. Travel down Colonial to Main Street.

The **Schoolhouse Museum** (4) is situated on the right corner. Its belltower is the only remaining section of the original schoolhouse, which was built in 1828. The building, administered by the Martha's Vineyard Historical Preservation Society, houses historic artifacts from the whaling era. It is open during the summer Monday through Friday from 10 to 2.

5 Turn left onto Main Street.

6 Take your next right, onto Owen Park Road.

Owen Park (6) contains benches, swings, and a bandstand that is used during Sunday evening concerts. Continue down the road to the public beach, where you can stop to swim and watch the ferries shuttle in and out of the harbor.

7 Return to Main Street, and turn right, heading toward West Chop. The road loops around, following the coastline.

West Chop, the Vineyard's northernmost headland, refers both to a geographical section of the island and to a self-contained community with its own beaches, tennis courts, and post office.

In the late nineteenth century, West Chop developed from a sheep pasture to a resort community. In 1872, two sea captains purchased a large tract of land for $400. As good at business as at sailing, the captains sold the land a few weeks later for $10,000. Fifteen years later, the West Chop Land and Wharf Company turned the area into an exclusive summer resort, transporting residents from the mainland to the

14 This road continues for a little more than a mile. Some sections are easier to navigate than others. Once you reach the peninsula, the dirt will turn to sand and you may have to walk your bike.

Herring Creek Beach

You can choose where along this lovely beach you want to sun and swim.

If you turn left, you'll head toward the shores of Lake Tashmoo. Be careful not to disturb the least terns that are nesting in the sand. Do not attempt to swim in the channel: the water is deep and the current is very strong. Do look across the channel to see if the eagle-like osprey is perched on its pole, scanning the sea for a tasty tidbit. Perhaps you'll watch it land in the water feet-first as it goes after its prey.

If you turn right, you'll soon be on the lifeguard-supervised beach that faces Vineyard Sound. From this beach, you'll have the same spectacular panorama as at West Chop, including two of the Elizabeth Islands—the largest, Naushon, and tiny Nonamesset. You'll also see Woods Hole and Falmouth on Cape Cod.

RETURN DIRECTIONS

15 Retrace your ride on the dirt road, turning left onto Daggett Street.

16 Ride down Daggett to Franklin Street. Turn right.

17 Remain on Franklin Street for eight blocks, until you reach Center Street.

> The **Association Hall Cemetery**, at the corner of Franklin and Center, has stones that mark the graves of Martha's Vineyard's English settlers. The oldest stone is dated 1770, but most represent the years 1805 to 1817.

18 Continue on Franklin for another block. Turn left onto Spring Street.

7. To Tisbury Meadow, Wompesket, and Ripley's Field Preserves

from Edgartown

Once you reach the three preserves, you can explore them either on bike or on foot. A guide for exploring Tisbury Meadow, Wompesket, and Ripley's Field Preserves appears in Chapter 25, page 139.

Round-trip biking distance from Edgartown: 16 miles

Terrain: Flat; 2 miles of unpaved road.

Food and drink: EDGARTOWN: A&P Supermarket; Healthy Gourmet Natural Food Market.
TISBURY: Scottish Bakehouse.

Restrooms: EDGARTOWN: In the Tourist Center on Church Street, between Main Street and Pease's Point Way.

Vineyard Haven bikers: Follow the directions in Chapter 8 until you reach the Tashmoo Overlook at direction #8. Proceed another 0.4 miles to Tisbury Meadow, which is on the left, and pick up the directions for this chapter. On your return, follow the directions until direction #14 and then turn left toward Vineyard Haven.

Oak Bluffs bikers: Follow the directions in Chapter 13 until you reach the blinker at direction #6. Then turn to direction #4 in this chapter. For your return, follow the directions in Chapter 13 to Oak Bluffs from Vineyard Haven.

8 Bike through the forest for two miles, until you reach Old County Road. Turn right.

9 Old County Road ends at State Road. Turn right. You will follow State Road for 1.3 miles, until you reach Tisbury Meadow Preserve.

10 Less than a half mile from the Old County Road intersection, on the right side, is the sign for Chicama Vineyard.

Across the street is the brightly painted sign for **Solviva**, a unique solar greenhouse in which 32 varieties of salad leaves, herbs, and edible flowers are grown. The greenhouse, open to the public on Sunday and Wednesday afternoons from 3 to 5, harnesses the sun's energy to heat the water wall that warms the greenhouse during the night. On very cold days, the heat that is emitted by the chickens who reside behind the water wall warms the greenhouse and prevents frost from nipping the delicate greens. Workers pluck leaves from the lettuce heads, wash them, seal them in plastic bags, and ship them to restaurants, where the menus boast that their salad greens were grown on Martha's Vineyard. Just ahead, on the left, the Scottish Bakehouse bakes scones, shortbreads, and other pastries.

11 Keep your eyes open for a meadow on the right. After the meadow, you'll see a driveway that leads to a house and the sign for **Tisbury Meadow Preserve**. Bike into the parking lot. The bike rack is located adjacent to the caretaker's cottage.

If you would like to explore Tisbury Meadow, Wompesket, and Ripley's Field Preserves on foot, see Chapter 25, page 139.

RETURN DIRECTIONS

12 Turn right on State Road and pedal for less than a mile until you see, on the left, the signs for Chicama Vineyard and Thimble Farm.

8. To Christiantown and Cedar Tree Neck Wildlife Sanctuary

from Vineyard Haven

This bike ride travels through the rural northern side of Martha's Vineyard, with its many farms, rolling hills, and rocky roads. Chapter 26, page 148, describes Christiantown and Christiantown Woods Preserve, and Chapter 27, page 151, explores Cedar Tree Neck Wildlife Sanctuary.

Round-trip biking distance from Vineyard Haven: 15 miles

Terrain: Moderately hilly; 1.7 miles of unpaved roads

Food and drink: VINEYARD HAVEN: Mad Martha's; Scottish Bakehouse.
   WEST TISBURY: Cronig's Up-Island Market.

Restrooms: VINEYARD HAVEN: (1) On the left, at the end of Union Street, as you disembark from the Steamship Authority Ferry; (2) At the far end of the A&P parking lot, on Water Street, the first street on the left after exiting from the ferry.

Edgartown bikers: Follow the directions in Chapter 7 to direction #9. Turn *left* at State Road, and pick up the directions in this chapter at direction #9.

Oak Bluffs bikers: Follow the signs to Vineyard Haven and pick up the directions in this chapter at direction #2.

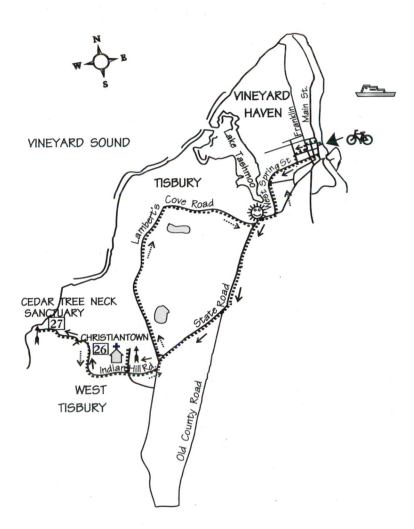

**FROM VINEYARD HAVEN TO CHRISTIANTOWN AND
CEDAR TREE NECK WILDLIFE SANCTUARY**

15 Indian Hill Road ends at State Road. Turn left.

16 Take your next left at Lambert's Cove Road.

This road curves around to **Lambert's Cove**, once a thriving fishing and farming community, which had its own ferry to Woods Hole. Although this loop is a mile longer than your original route on State Road, and has more hills, it is worth the extra exertion, since it is more scenic. Several freshwater ponds appear on the right. The first one is Seth's Pond, a favorite ice-skating area for Vineyard residents.

Also on the right, just past the sign for the Tisbury–West Tisbury town line, lie the remains of the last cranberry bogs cultivated on the island. There once were many bogs on the Vineyard, but high transportation costs made it too difficult for the growers to compete with the cranberry producers on Cape Cod.

17 When you reach State Road, turn left.

18 Turn left onto West Spring Street. Remain on Spring, bearing left at the fork and continuing until you reach Main Street.

19 There is one-way traffic on Main Street. The street is usually congested, and it is safer for you to walk your bike. An even better alternative is to park your bike in the rack and treat yourself to a caloric snack at one of the many shops that line the street.

9. To Long Point Wildlife Refuge

from Edgartown

"**N**o gain without pain" or "Seek and ye shall *finally* find" would be appropriate phrases to describe an excursion to Long Point Wildlife Refuge, one of my favorite places on Martha's Vineyard. Why should you travel down three miles of narrow, bumpy, unpaved road to reach Long Point? At the end lies a magnificent, relatively secluded south-coast beach bordered by several ponds and coves.

To explore Long Point Wildlife Refuge on foot, see Chapter 28, page 157.

Round-trip biking distance from Edgartown: 15 miles

Terrain: Flat; 3 miles of unpaved road

Food and drink: EDGARTOWN: Midway Market; Soigné; Morning Glory Farm.

Restrooms: EDGARTOWN: In the Visitors' Center, on Church Street between Main Street and Pease's Point Way.
LONG POINT: At the far end of the parking lot, on the left side.

Vineyard Haven bikers: Follow the directions in Chapter 1 until you reach the "blinker," at direction #5. Turn right onto Barnes Road and remain on it until reaching the Edgartown–West Tisbury Road. Turn right, and begin the directions for this chapter at direction #4.

Oak Bluffs bikers: Follow the directions in Chapter 10 until direction #11. Then pick up the directions below at direction #4.

4 Just beyond the bike path–Barnes Road intersection, on the left side of the Edgartown–West Tisbury Road, stands the **Mayhew Monument**, also referred to as the **Place by the Wayside**.

At this spot, in 1647, Reverend Thomas Mayhew, Jr., delivered his last sermon to the recently converted Wampanoag tribe before he set out on his ill-fated journey to England. As a tribute to Mayhew, members of the tribe placed a stone on this spot whenever they passed by. The stones were later replaced by this monument.

5 Pass the main entrance to the airport. Remain on the bike path, and pedal 0.3 miles to the second dirt road on the left.

6 Turn left onto this road, named Waldron's Bottom Road. (However, if you are visiting Long Point during the off-season— from mid-September to mid-June—travel another 0.8 miles, turn left onto Deep Bottom Road, and follow the signs to the refuge.)

7 During the summer season, follow Waldron's Bottom Road for 1.3 miles, until you see the Trustees of Reservations sign that directs you to turn left for the **Long Point Wildlife Refuge**. The sign will indicate if the parking lot is full.

8 Continue to follow the dirt road, forking right onto the road with the iron gate. Pedal for 1.25 miles to reach the refuge's parking lot, where an attendant will collect your entrance fee.

If you would like to explore the Long Point Wildlife Refuge on foot, see Chapter 28, page 157.

RETURN DIRECTIONS

9 From the parking lot, retrace your route down Hughe's Thumb Road.

10 At the "T" intersection, hook a left, followed by a quick right.

10. To Sepiessa Point Reservation

from Oak Bluffs

In 1991, the Martha's Vineyard Land Bank guaranteed public access to Tisbury Great Pond by purchasing Sepiessa Point, which lies between Tiah's Cove and Tississa Cove in West Tisbury. These coves are two in a series of ponds and coves that span the southern side of Martha's Vineyard and are separated from the Atlantic Ocean by narrow barrier beaches.

You can explore this property by land or water. There are hiking trails leading to a half-mile-long sandy beach that encompasses Sepiessa Point and faces the pond and ocean. Bring your bathing suit and beach shoes. A guide for exploring Sepiessa Point on foot appears in Chapter 29, page 161.

Round-trip biking distance from Oak Bluffs: 21 miles

Terrain: A few short hills

Food and drink: OAK BLUFFS: Nancy's Snack Bar; Mad Martha's; Cozy's; Subway.

Restrooms: OAK BLUFFS: On the left side of the Steamship Authority Wharf, as you face the terminal building on Beach Road.

Edgartown bikers: Follow the directions in Chapter 9 until you reach the access road to Long Point. Pick up the directions below at direction #11.

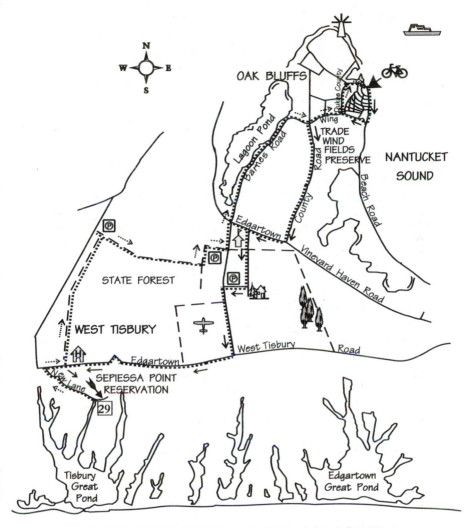

**FROM OAK BLUFFS TO SEPIESSA POINT
RESERVATION**

12 After passing the back yard of the youth hostel, proceed until the path makes a sharp right turn. At this point, turn *left,* in order to access the Edgartown–West Tisbury Road.

13 Turn right on the road and bike past the tiny fire station.

14 Turn left onto New Lane, the first paved road after the fire station.

15 Remain on New Lane, which becomes Tiah's Cove Road, for 1.2 miles, until you reach Sepiessa Point Reservation, on the right side of the road. The parking lot and bike rack are down the short dirt road.

If you would like to explore Sepiessa Point Reservation on foot, see Chapter 29, page 161.

RETURN DIRECTIONS

16 Follow the dirt road back out to New Lane.

17 Turn left onto New Lane.

18 At the junction with the Edgartown–West Tisbury Road, turn right, toward Edgartown.

19 Remain on this road until you turn left, toward the youth hostel, to access the bike trail.

20 The return trip follows the western edge of the State Forest. Proceed north—straight ahead—on the path for almost two miles.

21 When you reach the barrier and a small parking area, turn right onto the two-mile path that travels east through the forest.

22 At the "T" intersection, turn left. The path runs north for a half mile and then turns east for another half mile.

11. To Mill Brook Woods Preserve and Waskosim's Rock Reservation

from Edgartown

This trip offers a good workout and pleasant biking, with no extreme physical challenges. The trip returns via the quaint center of West Tisbury.

A guide for exploring Mill Brook Woods Preserve and Waskosim's Rock Reservation appears in Chapter 30, page 165.

Round-trip biking distance from Edgartown: 24 miles

Terrain: Mainly flat; paved roads only

Food and drink: EDGARTOWN: The Fresh Pasta Shoppe; A&P Supermarket; Healthy Gourmet.

WEST TISBURY: Cronig's Up-Island Market; Roadhouse Restaurant; The Vineyard Food Shop; Alley's General Store.

Restrooms: EDGARTOWN: In the Visitors' Center, on Church Street between Main Street and Pease's Point Way.

Vineyard Haven bikers: Follow the directions in Chapter 12 up to direction #11.

Oak Bluffs bikers: Follow the directions in Chapter 13 up to direction #6. Pick up the directions below at direction #4.

BIKING DIRECTIONS

1 Begin the trip on the Main Street side of Cannonball Park, also known as Memorial Park. This triangular park, with

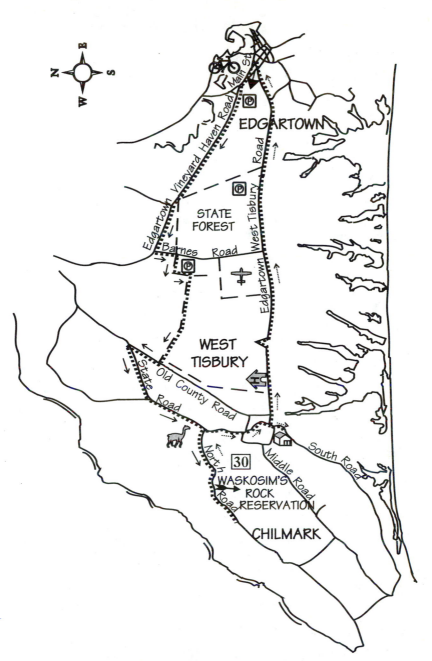

**FROM EDGARTOWN TO MILL BROOK WOODS
PRESERVE AND WASKOSIM'S ROCK RESERVATION**

Edgartown. However, if you feel the need for sustenance, turn right, toward the center of West Tisbury, a town that continues to reflect its origins as a rural farming village.

If you take the right turn toward **West Tisbury**, the Agricultural Hall, site of the annual County Fair in August, will loom ahead on the right. Nearby, the inviting porch in front of Alley's General Store entices travelers to stop and relax. Upon entering Alley's, whose sign boasts ''Dealers in Almost Everything,'' one is transported a hundred years back to the pre-supermarket era, when the general store both supplied provisions and was the center of a community's social life.

Back Alley's, at the rear of the parking lot, is a cafe that sells takeout food.

Across the street is the **Field Gallery**, whose delightful sculptures by Tom Maley scamper across the grounds.

14 To return to Edgartown from the Field Gallery, turn right to rejoin the Edgartown–West Tisbury Road.

15 At the fork, keep to the right, remaining on the Edgartown–West Tisbury Road for the rest of the nine-mile trip.

Almost immediately past West Tisbury, on your left, is the charming Mill Pond, which is often surrounded by ducks and swans patiently waiting for generous travelers to stop and feed them.

A half mile further, on the left, sits the Manter Youth Hostel. It provides rooms and cooking facilities for cyclists, who are limited to a three-day stay.

16 The bike path begins behind the youth hostel. To access the path, cut across the playing field adjacent to the hostel. The path lies directly behind the field.

17 Go right, to the east, on the path. This hilly and scenic route wends its way through the forest. Although the path is

12. To Fulling Mill Brook Preserve and Middle Road Sanctuary

from Vineyard Haven

This trip reveals the undeveloped up-island landscape. Zoning rules have helped retain the rural character of the western half of the island.

A guide to exploring Fulling Mill Brook Preserve and Middle Road Sanctuary on foot appears in Chapter 31, page 169.

Round-trip biking distance from Vineyard Haven: 19 miles

Terrain: Several short hills

Food and drink: VINEYARD HAVEN: A&P Supermarket; Black Dog Bakery; Mad Martha's.

WEST TISBURY: Cronig's Up-Island Market; Vineyard Food Shop; Roadhouse Restaurant.

Restrooms: VINEYARD HAVEN: (1) In the building on the left side of the Steamship Authority Ferry Wharf; (2) At the far end of the A&P parking lot on Water Street.

Edgartown bikers: Follow the directions in Chapter 11 up to direction #9. Pick up this chapter at direction #9.

Oak Bluffs bikers: Follow the directions in Chapter 13 up to direction #13.

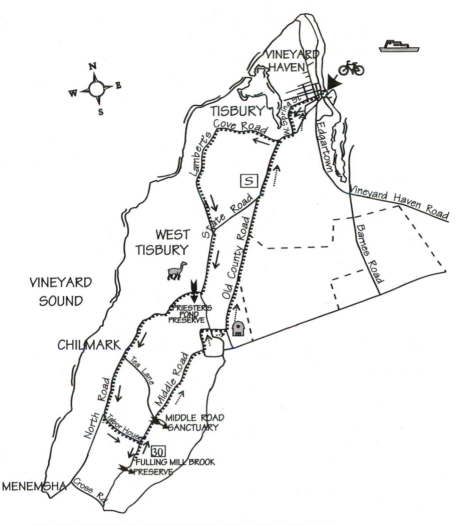

**FROM VINEYARD HAVEN TO FULLING MILL BROOK
PRESERVE AND MIDDLE ROAD SANCTUARY**

If you would like to explore Middle Road Sanctuary on foot, see Chapter 31, page 169.

RETURN DIRECTIONS

14 From the entrance to Middle Road Sanctuary, turn right onto Middle Road. Bike for about two miles over hilly terrain with scenery reminiscent of northern Vermont.

15 At the "T" intersection, turn left onto Panhandle Road.

16 Follow Panhandle 0.7 miles, as it bends sharply to the right and crosses the intersection with State Road. At the "T" intersection with Old County Road, turn left. The Granary Gallery appears on the right.

17 Pedal on Old County for almost three miles, until it ends at State Road. Turn right.

Just ahead on the left is the sign for **Solviva**, a solar greenhouse that grows 32 varieties of salad leaves, herbs, and edible flowers. The greenhouse, open to the public Sunday and Wednesday afternoons from 3 to 5, contains a solar-heated water wall that provides heat during the winter. On very cold days, heat emitted from the chickens that live in coops behind the water wall provides enough warmth to prevent the delicate greens from being nipped by frost.

18 Remain on State Road for 1.6 miles. Immediately after the Lake Tashmoo Overlook, take the left onto West Spring Street.

19 Follow West Spring as it bends right and merges with Spring Street. Remain on Spring as it descends to Main Street.

20 Turn left onto Main.

21 Turn right onto Union Street, which passes Mad Martha's ice cream shop and ends at the Steamship Authority Wharf.

13. To Menemsha and Menemsha Hills Reservation

from Oak Bluffs

This bike ride, combined with stops at Menemsha and Menemsha Hills Reservation, makes for a terrific day-trip.

A guide to exploring Menemsha and Menemsha Hills Reservation on foot appears in Chapter 32, page 175.

Round-trip biking distance from Oak Bluffs: 28 miles

Terrain: Hilly

Food and drink: OAK BLUFFS: Reliable Self-Service Market; Subway; Nancy's Snack Bar.
   MENEMSHA: Galley Snack Bar; Home Port Restaurant.
   VINEYARD HAVEN: Portside Restaurant.

Restrooms: OAK BLUFFS: (1) On the right-hand corner of Seaview Avenue, as you disembark from the Steamship Authority Ferry. (2) In the pedestrian mall between Circuit and Kennebec Avenues, near the post office and bike rack.
   MENEMSHA: On Basin Road, across from the fish markets.

Vineyard Haven bikers: Bike two miles out of Vineyard Haven along the Edgartown–Vineyard Haven Road. At the "blinker," at the intersection of Barnes Road, turn right. Pick up the directions below at direction #6.

Edgartown bikers: Bike four and a half miles down the Edgartown–Vineyard Haven Road. At the "blinker," at Barnes Road, turn left. Pick up the directions below at direction #6.

7 A half mile past the "blinker," and just after the sign for the Oak Bluffs–Edgartown town line, is the bicycle entrance to the State Forest. Turn right onto the bike path.

8 The path travels west for a half mile and then swings south for another half mile. The 365-acre Greenlands conservation area is on the right.

9 Another bike path emerges from the west. *Don't miss* the right turn onto this path. You will bike along it for two miles through the forest, toward West Tisbury and the youth hostel.

10 The two-mile stretch through the forest ends at a barrier. Proceed past the barrier into the parking area. Before you reach the road, turn left, onto the continuation of the bike path. Remain on the path, which parallels Old County Road, for one mile.

11 When the bike path begins to angle away from the road, leave the path, join the road, and continue pedaling south.

12 Stay on Old County Road until you spot, on the left, a large barn that houses the Granary Gallery and Red Barn Emporium. Turn right onto Scotchmans Bridge, the street across from the Red Barn. (There probably is no street sign at this corner.)

13 Travel down this rustic country road, through the intersection with State Road. The road hooks left and continues for a half mile.

14 After passing a wildlife refuge on your right, a paved road, which again may not have a street sign, will emerge, also on the right. This is Middle Road, so called because it runs down the center of the island. Turn onto Middle Road. To reach Menemsha and the Menemsha Hills Reservation, you will follow Middle Road for its entire 4.3-mile length.

Although a taxing ride because of the hills, Middle Road is my favorite island road. I enjoy looking at the Tiasquam

reach Tisbury) for 8.5 miles, until you reach West Spring Street in Vineyard Haven.

North Road parallels Middle Road. South Road, another road on the southern side of the island, also travels in the same direction. I avoid biking on South Road because it is narrow, curvy, and hilly, with a lot of traffic and no bike path. Middle Road is the least busy. I prefer North Road for the return route because it is straighter and less hilly. It soon will have a bike path along the stretch from Menemsha to Tisbury.

This return route emphasizes the dramatic physical differences among the island towns, from heavily wooded Chilmark to the rolling farmland of West Tisbury. Once you reach Tisbury, of which Vineyard Haven is a part, you'll find a more commercial atmosphere.

20 Bear left at the junction with State Road, following the signs to Vineyard Haven.

Takemmy Farm lies just past the junction, on the left. Yes, those animals *are* llamas. You can visit them on Wednesday and Saturday afternoons. If you bike up the road leading into the farm, you'll find a stand that sells items produced on the farm. Don't look for an attendant. You simply make your choice and leave the money in the cash register.

After Takemmy Farm, continue traveling toward Vineyard Haven.

21 After cycling three miles from the junction with State Road, look on the left for the **Lake Tashmoo Overlook**. You can stop and admire Lake Tashmoo and Vineyard Sound.

22 Immediately after the overlook, turn left onto West Spring Street. Although this route through Vineyard Haven is longer, it avoids the congestion on State Road.

23 Follow West Spring as it swings around, eventually merging

14. To Gay Head Cliffs and Beach and Lobsterville

from Vineyard Haven

This trip from Vineyard Haven to Gay Head and back, spanning twenty miles in each direction, is the most strenuous but also the most rewarding in this book.

> The rolling terrain creates the strain
> But don't complain; there is much to gain
> From the scenery, which, in the main, lessens the pain!

In order to reach Gay Head, you must bike through Chilmark, where the landscape resembles northern New England. The rolling hills and antique farmhouses, the large oak and maple trees shading the road, and the rural character of the countryside and town are more like Vermont than a typical island resort community.

A guide to exploring Gay Head Cliffs and Beach on foot appears in Chapter 33, page 179.

Round-trip biking distance from Vineyard Haven: 40 miles

Terrain: Hilly

Food and drink: VINEYARD HAVEN: A&P Supermarket; Black Dog Bakery.
CHILMARK: Chilmark Chocolates; Chilmark Store.
GAY HEAD: Aquinnah.
WEST TISBURY: Roadhouse Restaurant; Vineyard Food Shop; Cronig's Down-Island Market.

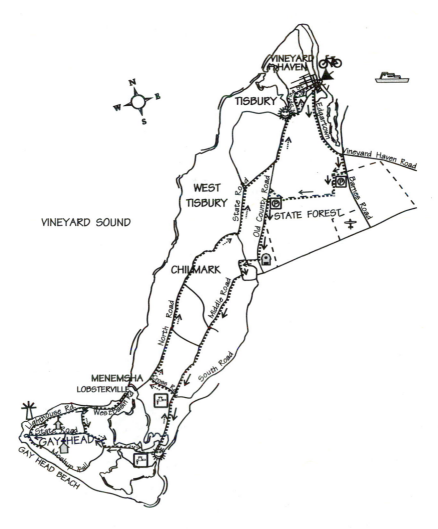

**FROM VINEYARD HAVEN TO GAY HEAD CLIFFS AND
BEACH AND LOBSTERVILLE**

14 Just after the refuge, *don't miss* turning right onto the first paved road. This is Middle Road. Again, it is unlikely that you will see a street sign.

15 Remain on scenic Middle Road, ascending and descending for 4.3 miles, until you reach Chilmark Center, at the junction of Middle Road, Menemsha Cross Road, and South Road.

The name of this intersection, Beetlebung Corner, is derived from the early settlers' use of tupelo trees. Colonists used the tough, dense wood from tupelo trees for making wooden mallets or "beetles." Because this wood absorbs less water than the wood from other island trees, it was also used for making "bungs"—corks—for plugging the holes in barrels. These "bungs" were then hammered in by the "beetles." The "beetlebung" trees stand to your left when you reach this intersection.

16 Continue straight onto South Road, toward Gay Head.

If you need to refill your water bottle, you'll find a hose to the right of the Chilmark Store, on the right side of the street. This shop sells a variety of foodstuffs.

If you really want an energy boost, head for Chilmark Chocolates, just down the road on the right. This store, which makes and sells the best chocolates I've ever eaten, is certainly worth a visit. The owners are committed to employing people with disabilities. When you enter the shop, you will be dazzled by the array of confections, but don't forget to look through the window on your right to watch the candy-making process. If the sugar makes you thirsty, there is a water faucet to the right of the deck. Biking the many miles to Gay Head ensures a guilt-free stop at this unique establishment.

17 Remain on this arduous but scenic stretch of South Road for seven miles.

RETURN DIRECTIONS

22 The return trip cuts across the north side of the island. From the beach, pedal back toward the parking lot, cross South Road, and bear right onto Lighthouse Road. This two-mile stretch parallels South Road. If you continue past the junction with Lobsterville Road and travel straight for another mile and a half, you will pass through **Lobsterville** to Menemsha Basin.

One hundred years ago, before the creation of Menemsha Harbor, Lobsterville was the most important fishing village on Martha's Vineyard. Ships from New York made daily visits to purchase fish and lobster. Now the village no longer exists, and the area is used for beaching, fishing, and enjoying the views of Menemsha Harbor and Menemsha Pond.

On the way to this former harbor, you pass **Lobsterville Beach**, part of the Gay Head Indian Reserve and open to the public. If you want to stop and swim, wheel your bike onto the beach and jump in.

The Cranberry Lands, across from the beach, are covered with wild roses, bayberry bushes, and cranberries, favorites both of birds and birdwatchers.

The road ends at Menemsha Basin. Across the channel sits the quaint village of Menemsha, a thriving fishing port and home of many of the vessels whose owners continue to earn their living from the sea.

If you look north out into the ocean you'll have a terrific view of Naushon, the largest Elizabeth Island.

23 To return to South Road, retrace your route on West Basin Road until you reach Lobsterville Road. Turn left onto Lobsterville Road.

24 You'll soon come to a "T" intersection at South Road. Turn left onto South Road, and travel three and a half miles to Beetlebung Corner.

Part Two

ON FOOT

15. Edgartown and Lighthouse Beach

"Edgartown from Land and Sea" would be an apt title for this historical tour through the heart of Edgartown and on to Lighthouse Beach and Eel Pond. The narrow streets of Edgartown, lined with meticulously landscaped, spacious old homes, are reminiscent of the nineteenth century, when the town was a prosperous whaling community.

Lighthouse Beach is a five-minute walk from the center of town. From the coastline you'll have a fine view of the elegant Edgartown residences as well as a panorama of Edgartown Harbor, Chappaquiddick, and Cape Poge. At unspoiled Lighthouse Beach you can swim or picnic while watching windsurfers race across the yacht-filled harbor.

The streets in the heart of Edgartown are narrow; traffic can flow in only one direction. Biking is not permitted on the major streets, so you must either walk your bike or park it in one of the bike racks along the way. A convenient rack is on Pease's Point Way. (Take the second left after Cannonball Park and then the first right.) There are other bike racks in the town's business district, but there is no rack at Lighthouse Beach.

If you are arriving by car, save yourself the aggravation of hunting for a parking place and then worrying about the time, by parking in the free outlying lots. One lot is near the Triangle intersection and the other is on Robinson Road. A trolley frequently shuttles passengers between the town and the lots.

For food and drink during your walk, try: Among the Flowers Cafe, on Mayhew Lane; the Wharf Pub, on Main Street near the harbor; Mad Martha's, on North Water Street; or Mrs. Miller's

EDGARTOWN AND LIGHTHOUSE BEACH

The first house belonged to Thomas Cooke, a businessman and the Edgartown customs collector, who built this residence in 1765 to house his office and family. Much of the twelve-room house, including many of the window panes, remains unchanged. Inside are relics from the island's past, including costumes, dolls, and whaling artifacts.

Two other buildings stand on the Society's grounds. The Gale Huntington Library of History and the Francis Foster Museum are located in the main building. Inside the library hangs a portrait of wealthy Dr. Fisher. Thousands of books on Vineyard history and more than one hundred logbooks from whaling vessels line the walls. The museum contains scrimshaw, ship models, paintings, and even marble headstones from the graves of two favorite chickens that belonged to Nancy Luce, an eccentric former resident of West Tisbury.

The third building is a carriage shed housing a hand-pumped fire engine, a peddler's cart, a racing boat, and a Nomans Land boat.

The brick tower in the middle of the lawn holds the gigantic Fresnel lens from the old Gay Head Lighthouse. The lens is lit each night, and on Sunday evenings in the summer the lens rotates as it did hundreds of years ago, generating a beacon that can be seen for twenty miles.

Go east on Cooke Street toward the waterfront. On the left side where Summer Street intersects Cooke Street stands the Baylies-designed **Federated Church** (6), built in 1828. Congregational services are held each Sunday in its spartan sanctuary, the oldest on the island. Go inside to see the hanging whale-oil lamps, the old organ, and the enclosed pews that were designed to trap the heat during cold winter months.

Continue on Cooke Street for another block until you reach South Water Street. Turn left and walk for a short one and a half blocks until you reach number 9, the house built by Captain Thomas Milton, a sea captain who, after retiring, grew wealthy from his investments in Edgartown real estate. In 1840 he built this house next to the flame tree that he had brought back from a trip to the Orient seven years earlier. This huge and handsome tree is known as the **pagoda tree** (7) and is said to be the oldest one on this continent.

proper sense of proportion, and elegant architectural details of these captains' homes combine to create one of the most aesthetically pleasing avenues on the Vineyard. Number 86, which belonged to Captain Jared Fisher, is one of the loveliest homes. Its Greek Revival style indicates that it was built at the same time as the Daniel Fisher House. Look up at the widow's walk for the patient wife who continues to peer through her spyglass for her husband's overdue ship.

Peek into the sides and backyards of these homes to see the carefully cultivated gardens where a variety of colorful blooms thrive in the salt air.

The imposing building situated on the corner of North Water Street and Starbuck Neck Road is the Harbor View Hotel, a popular site for summer weddings. Across the street from the hotel is a path leading to the lighthouse.

Follow the path to the **Edgartown Lighthouse**, located at the entrance to Edgartown Harbor. Originally the lighthouse was built on a manmade island of granite blocks and was connected by a wooden walkway to the mainland. The walkway was replaced by a causeway, which became unnecessary when ocean currents created a small barrier beach and a sandy access strip.

The seascape to your right reveals magnificent yachts anchored in the harbor, sailboats racing across the bay, and windsurfers' brightly colored sails weaving among the stately vessels. You will also spot the *On Time* ferries shuttling back and forth to Chappaquiddick. The view toward Chappaquiddick includes bathers, fishermen, and numerous homes perched on the bluffs.

As you walk down the mile-long stretch toward Eel Pond, you'll have a closer view of narrow Cape Poge. This isolated peninsula is accessible only by boat or by driving seven miles on a soft, sandy beach. The abundance of fish in Cape Poge Bay draws not only fishermen but also flocks of seagulls who breed on the uninhabited western tip. If you make the trip to Cape Poge in June, beware of dive-bombing mother gulls protecting their young.

On your left is Eel Pond, a favorite island spot for shellfishing. Among the varieties of shells found on the beach are hard,

16. Sheriff's Meadow Sanctuary

Even though it is located in the heart of Edgartown, this small sanctuary has a range of natural communities usually found miles from civilization. Here you'll find meadow and woodland, freshwater pond and saltwater marsh—diverse habitats supporting a wide variety of flora and fauna. The trail winds through lush foliage and allows views across Eel Pond to Nantucket Sound and Chappaquiddick. Perhaps because Sheriff's Meadow is so near the hustle and bustle of Edgartown, the variety and number of bird calls is all the more noticeable. Bring your binoculars so you can spot such birds as black-bellied plovers, red-winged blackbirds, or great blue herons. You may also encounter a raccoon crawling through the brush or spy several swans flying from one body of water to the next.

DIRECTIONS: *To reach the sanctuary from the Main Street side of Cannonball Park in Edgartown, turn left onto Pease's Point Way. Continue straight on Pease's Point Way onto Planting Field Way. Proceed 0.2 miles down Planting Field Way. Look for a small Sheriff's Meadow sign on the right side of the road.*

Hiking time: 30 minutes

Much of the land in this 17-acre sanctuary originally belonged to Henry Beetle Hough, an influential and respected island resident who for many years was editor and publisher of the weekly newspaper, the *Vineyard Gazette.* In order to protect this property from future development, Henry and his wife, Betty, created the Sheriff's Meadow Foundation in 1958, donating eleven acres of the land that surrounds Sheriff's Pond. During

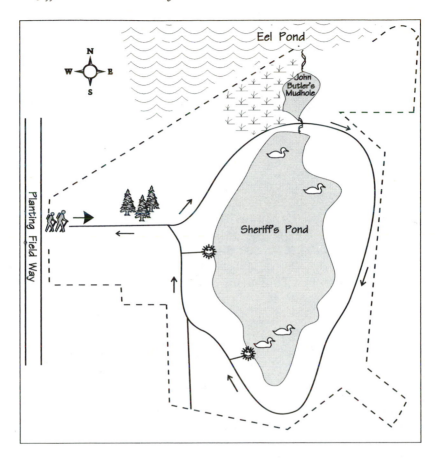

SHERIFF'S MEADOW SANCTUARY

notice that the vegetation is very dense. **Pasture rose** and **multiflora rose** reach out into the path, hooking the unsuspecting hiker with their thorny branches.

Along this stretch, nonnative plant species, with their jungle-like density of vines, stems, and runners, are crowding out native species. The Sheriff's Meadow Foundation is attempting to reduce the numbers of the invaders, principally the Asiatic bittersweet, Japanese honeysuckle, and porcelain berry.

17. Caroline Tuthill Wildlife Preserve

The Caroline Tuthill Wildlife Preserve is just a stone's throw from the hustle and bustle of the Triangle shopping area, but its hiking trails through pine forest and meadow give it the feeling of being far removed from civilization. This preserve, administered by the low-profile Sheriff's Meadow Foundation, is one of Martha's Vineyard's hidden treasures. Even long-time residents are not aware of its hiking trails along the shore of scenic Sengekontacket Pond and the opportunities for birdwatching around the salt marsh. If you seek a spot to which you can bike in less than an hour or if you'd like to hike on a varied but not taxing terrain that is covered with blueberry and huckleberry bushes, then the Caroline Tuthill Wildlife Preserve is your destination.

DIRECTIONS: *From the Triangle intersection in Edgartown, travel 0.4 miles west on the Edgartown–Vineyard Haven Road.*

Hiking time: 40 minutes

The Sheriff's Meadow Foundation, a conservation agency that maintains natural habitats, oversees this preserve. Unlike the Land Bank, which displays its properties and wants people to use them, the Sheriff's Meadow properties are not as well-advertised, in hopes that they will not become overused. The Caroline Tuthill Wildlife Preserve consists of a one-and-a-half-mile trail that loops through 154 acres of woodlands, salt marsh, and fields.

As you walk through the preserve, you'll notice several chasm-like depressions in the ground. These are called kettle

Soon after you begin your hike you'll see evergreen sprouts on both sides of the trail. The sprouts are young pitch pine trees, which are found all over the island. Underneath the sprouts are pine tree stumps, and just below the stumps are large root systems. These large, vigorous roots are close to the surface of the ground. When pitch pine trees have been cut down or are destroyed by fire, they quickly issue new sprouts and reinstate themselves.

During the summer you'll likely spot a small ground-hugging wildflower that has five white petals and variegated leaves. This distinctive flower possesses a distinctive name: spotted pipsissewa.

At the fork, bear left and continue on the trail that winds through a grove of oaks and then through a grove of pines. As you walk, look down at the crunchy gray-blue moss-like clumps. These primitive organisms are a variety of lichens known as reindeer moss. They have no roots, stems, leaves, or flowers. Lichens, which have been around for millions of years, are composed of two kinds of organisms: fungi and algae. Both components work together like a well-coached team, performing different functions that allow survival in hot, arid regions as well as on frigid, wind-blown mountain tops. The fungi provide protection and supply moisture while the algae provide the food.

Lichens feel sharp and brittle if they grow in dry conditions or soft and spongy if they have absorbed water. If you have any extra water with you, put a piece of the dry lichen in a cup. Add a little water and watch as the lichen absorbs all the liquid. This nifty moisture-conservation trick is one reason lichens can survive droughts or extreme heat or cold. The reindeer moss may not mind heat or cold, but it is very fussy about air quality and refuses to grow in polluted areas. Vineyarders are partial to reindeer moss because it reinforces their belief that their unpolluted island is superior to the mainland.

Ignore the path emerging on the left and continue walking straight, watching for the yellow markers nailed to tree trunks.

The trail approaches Sengekontacket Pond and then bends to the right following the shore. Stop for a view of the pond, the beach, Nantucket Sound, and Beach Road. To the north you can

18. Felix Neck Wildlife Sanctuary

Felix Neck Wildlife Sanctuary, a Massachusetts Audubon Society property, provides an assortment of activities, from bird and wildlife identification walks to snorkeling and canoe trips. As you walk along wide, level trails through 350 acres of beach, marsh, open fields, and woodlands, you may encounter wild turkeys, Canada geese, ospreys, or even a horseshoe crab. Birders describe this scenic sanctuary as one of the prime island locales for observing wild native birds. Since Felix Neck is centrally located off the bike path on the Edgartown–Vineyard Haven Road, it is an ideal destination for the less-experienced or younger cyclist.

DIRECTIONS: *From the triangle intersection in Edgartown, travel 2.2 miles on the Edgartown–Vineyard Haven Road. From Vineyard Haven, the distance is 4.2 miles on the same road. An incised rectangular stone next to a Massachusetts Audubon Society sign marks the entrance to the sanctuary, on the right side of the road if coming from Edgartown. The sanctuary lies at the end of a half-mile-long dirt road.*

Bikers should proceed down the trail that begins on the left of the sandy road. This narrow path winds through a pine forest, brushes the ubiquitous huckleberry bushes, and crosses over pine tree roots, always paralleling the road.

Cross the dirt road into an open grassy area with two osprey poles straddling the path. Ospreys, which resemble eagles, prefer to nest on top of dead trees near fish-laden water. Due to a diminished number of available perches, the island osprey population has been greatly reduced. Gus Ben David, the director of Felix Neck, was instrumental in increasing the number of ospreys by encouraging the telephone company

Hiking time: 90 minutes

Felix Neck Wildlife Sanctuary is open daily, year-round, from 8 to 4. The adult entrance fee is $3; children are $2. Admission is free to members of the Massachusetts Audubon Society.

The Visitors' Center contains trail maps, a shop selling nature-oriented items, and an exhibit room with displays as well as freshwater and saltwater aquariums filled with native fish, bivalves, amphibians, and reptiles. A restroom is also located in the building. Outside under the barn you might spot nesting barn owls.

Felix Neck employs naturalists who offer a variety of birdwatching, canoeing, stargazing, and seashell-identifying excursions. The sanctuary also serves as a summer day camp for children ages seven to twelve. But its most important function is to provide a natural habitat for its many varied species of wildlife.

Before European settlers arrived on the Vineyard, this land was inhabited by Native Americans who farmed crops such as squash, tobacco, and Jerusalem artichokes. They called this section of the island Weenomset, which means "place of the grape." When the English arrived, they named the land after Felix Kuttashamaquat, a Native American who farmed and grazed his sheep here.

For the next three hundred years Felix Neck was owned and farmed by the Smith family. The Visitors' Center stands on the foundation of the Smith family's old horse barn. In 1963, Walter Smith sold 180 acres to George Moffett, with the understanding that Moffett would keep only 40 acres for himself and put the rest of the land in trust so that it would remain forever wild.

In 1964, Moffett gave the Martha's Vineyard Natural History Society permission to use the property for a nature-study program, which continues today and is called Fern and Feather. In 1969 Moffett donated the property to the Massachusetts Audubon Society. The Audubon Society acquired the additional 170 acres of the present sanctuary through other donations.

Begin your hike on the Yellow Trail, which starts behind the Visitors' Center. You will soon come to a wooden boardwalk

The water in Sengekontacket Pond is seeded for scallops and clams. During low tide you'll often see clammers raking up quahogs or digging for steamers. Keep your eyes to the ground as you stroll along the shore for clam, mussel, whelk, and scallop shells. You may also find the molt of a **horseshoe crab**. The molt, which looks like a dead horseshoe crab, is actually its cast-off shell. If you are not squeamish, pick up this strange-looking arthropod and look for the little slit that the crab used as an escape hatch. Horseshoe crabs, like ticks, are arachnids, prehistoric fauna that have been around since the time of the glacier.

If you venture into the water, check the bottom for mud snails, whose important function is to clean the water by eating the decaying organic matter that has settled on the pond's floor.

Unless the tide is very high, you can continue walking along the water's edge until you swing around and face north toward Beach Road and the Joseph A. Sylvia State Beach, which form a barrier between Sengekontacket Pond and Vineyard Sound. Soon you will reach a path emerging from the right. Hop onto this path, which is the continuation of the Yellow Trail.

During the summer months, watch for the brilliant orange flower called butterfly weed. Its name is derived from its frequent companion, the monarch butterfly, that dines on its clusters of five curved and five upright petals. This plant is also called pleurisy root, because the Native Americans chewed its roots to alleviate the lung condition we now know as pleurisy.

Continue on this path and pass the small building on the right that used to be the home of Clarence Smith. Clarence, one of the former landowners, lived as a hermit in this camp until his death. The building is now used as a classroom for the Fern and Feather Day Camp.

The Red Trail emerges just after another manmade body of water, named Elizabeth's Pond. Turn left onto the Red Trail.

This path travels through a pitch pine forest with an undercover of bayberry and huckleberry bushes. You'll notice that the trees and bushes are smaller and more deformed than in the other areas of Felix Neck. Because this land is higher and less protected, the continual bombardment of wind and salt spray has stunted the growth of the bushes and trees.

Cormorant

with the Jessica Hancock Trail, indicated by markers for the White Trail. This 15-minute loop runs next to the marsh and leads to the edge of Sengekontacket Pond for a close view of its eastern tip.

To return to the parking lot after exploring the White Trail, turn left onto the Orange Trail.

Unfortunately, the bridge has not been passable for more than a decade. As of this writing, the state of Massachusetts, the town of Edgartown, and the Trustees of Reservations have been negotiating when to reopen the bridge. The issue involved is the safety of the endangered piping plover, a sand-colored bird that inhabits the area. By the time of publication, the bridge may be open and East Beach may once again be accessible.

The Kennedy incident fueled Chappaquiddick's new notoriety, which, combined with the 1970s building boom, created a demand for homes that produced the first surge of population growth in one hundred years. Even today, people are more likely to associate this little island with the Kennedy tragedy than with its other considerable assets.

In order to get to Chappaquiddick, you must hop on the ferry that runs continually between Edgartown and Chappaquiddick, an Indian word meaning "the separated island." Chappaquiddick is not, in fact, an island: it is connected to Martha's Vineyard by a narrow barrier beach at its southern tip.

Once you reach Chappy, you'll discover there is not much happening on this scenic, no-frills "almost-island." Its residents enjoy the outdoor life and prefer communing with nature without any commercial interference. The five chapters that follow provide opportunities for visitors to experience the natural beauty of Chappaquiddick.

19. Brine's Pond Preserve

Brine's Pond is a conservation area owned and operated by the Martha's Vineyard Land Bank Commission. It features an island of beetlebung trees and a profusion of blueberry and huckleberry bushes.

Biking is permitted in the preserve.

DIRECTIONS: *From the ferry, travel 1.7 miles on Chappaquiddick Road.*

Hiking time: 30 minutes

Your first introduction to the preserve is an open field encircling a pristine pond. On closer inspection you will see an island populated by a grove of **beetlebung** trees. Beetlebung is the Vineyard name for the tupelo tree, the dense wood of which was used by the island's early settlers for the wooden "beetles" (mallets) that drove the "bungs" (corks) used to plug barrel holes.

The entrance to the preserve is to the left of the sign for the Chappaquiddick Community Center. If you come by bike, park your bike in the rack at the front of the property, near the road. To access the trail, walk straight ahead, keeping the pond on your left.

The windmill decorating the property was placed there by a previous owner who attempted to harness the wind to produce energy for his farm.

During your hike you will encounter an abundance of blueberry and huckleberry bushes. Both plants often grow beneath oak trees. Both have small oval leaves, with huckleberry

20. Chappy Five Corners Preserve

Chappy Five Corners Preserve, another property of the Martha's Vineyard Land Bank Commission, features a colorful wetland in the middle of a dense forest. It has an abundance of huckleberry and blueberry bushes.

Bikes are allowed in the preserve.

DIRECTIONS: *From the ferry, travel 3.3 miles on Chappaquiddick Road.*

Hiking time: 30 minutes

This 27-acre reservation is an interesting combination of forest and wetland. The forested area contains similar vegetation to the woods in Brine's Pond Preserve. Both are good examples of fallow-field succession, where certain varieties of plants over time are replaced by others. After a number of years of this gradual replacement, the entire community is changed.

During the eighteenth and nineteenth centuries this area was mainly grassland and was used as pasture for sheep and cattle. When the settlers turned from farming to whaling, the ungrazed land was receptive to a variety of small shrubs, such as huckleberry, blueberry, and bayberry, along with red cedar trees. Pitch pine trees succeeded red cedar, and the pine trees created enough shade for oak trees to get a foothold. The woods in Chappy Five Corners are filled with pine trees growing among white and black oak trees. Most Vineyard forests are at this same stage of succession.

Pitch pine   White oak

white blossoms. Maples and beetlebung trees flaunt their
rainbow of bright colors in the fall.

Cross the tiny wooden bridge over the wetland. The vine with
many tendrils that is attaching itself to anything in its path is
named greenbriar.

The trail then swings back into the forest and joins a dirt road.
Turn left. Continue on this road back to the parking area.

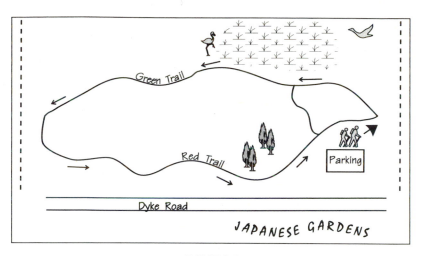

MYTOI

excavated to form the pond was used to build the small hills that
surround the garden. The gurgling brook originates from the
well near the Trustees' office building. The benches were
donated by Chappaquiddick residents.

Cross the footbridge to the island, where you can sit on the
wooden bench and watch the inhabitants of the pond. On the
water you'll see whirligig beetles swimming in their never-
ending circles while the water striders are busily jumping from
spot to spot. Look into the water for the goldfish and carp that
the Trustees stock every June. Kingfishers and ospreys looking
for a fish dinner often swoop down into the water. If you drop
bread crumbs into the pond, the snapping and painted turtles
will inch their way to the surface. The bright yellow markings on
the head and neck of the painted turtle distinguish it from the
snapping turtle.

To explore the rest of the sanctuary, cross Dyke Road and pick
up the trail that winds through the pitch pine forest down to the
salt marsh. The paths are marked with Trustees of Reservations
insignias that are nailed to trees.

The Green Trail begins across from the main entrance to
Mytoi. The trail winds down to the salt marsh and has several

22. Poucha Pond Reservation

Poucha Pond Reservation features trails that wind through open fields, woods, and marshland until they reach the pond itself, a body of water that extends from Chappaquiddick's famous Dyke Bridge to remote Wasque Point. Many species of birds come to feast on the abundant fish and crustaceans that inhabit the marsh and pond.

Although the property, owned and administered by the Martha's Vineyard Land Bank, abuts Poucha Pond, there are no bathing beaches. Biking and picnicking are allowed. If the sight of all that water makes you thirst for a swim, bike or walk a mile up the road to Wasque Reservation (see Chapter 23).

DIRECTIONS: *Poucha Pond is 3.8 miles from the Chappaquiddick ferry. From the ferry, travel on Chappaquiddick Road, following it as it bends sharply to the right. When it ends, at Wasque Road, turn left. The reservation is ahead, on the left, next to Wasque Farm.*

Hiking time: 1 hour

During the last three hundred years Martha's Vineyard's settlers have found many uses for this remote property. At one time Poucha Pond was open to the sea and was used as a harbor. However, by 1722 the tides and currents had filled the opening with sand.

In 1845, landowners constructed a dike to control the flow of water into and out of the pond. Each winter they flooded the pond with fresh water, and in the spring they opened the dike's gates so the herring and shad could swim into the pond and deposit their eggs. Fishermen then caught the fish, which they pickled, salted, and shipped in barrels to New York.

the young pine trees growing along the edges of the trail. Whenever land is cleared, the cut pines quickly reappear, because their large root systems lie just below the ground ready to sprout new trees.

After leaving the pine forest, you'll hike through a woodland filled with oak trees. Years ago, this section was probably inhabited by pine trees. However, once the oak trees took hold, they overshadowed the pines, causing them to weaken and die. You can calculate how many years have elapsed since the land was farmed by noting what type of vegetation is occupying the area. Open fields on the Vineyard often sprout red cedar trees, followed by woody shrubs like huckleberry and blueberry. Pitch pine trees follow and the last variety of tree in the order of succession is the oak.

The closer you get to the water, the more gnarled and deformed are the trees, victims of the strong winds that bombard the eastern side of the island. Throughout the hike you'll also see a number of fallen trees, victims of Hurricane Bob, which blasted the Vineyard in August 1991.

At the fork, continue to follow the Red Trail.

At the intersection with the Blue Trail, bear right and follow the Blue Trail through the salt marsh. You'll find the groundsel tree, also called the high tide bush, growing at the edge of the marsh. It's easiest to spot this shrub in the autumn, when the seeds on the female plant mature into small, white, feathery clusters.

This trail leads to several pond and marsh lookouts, good vantage points to look for common and least terns, which fish the shallow water for minnows. You may also see great black-backed and herring gulls, which are responsible for the broken shells you see on the ground. The gulls pull the shellfish out of the water, fly into the air, and drop the shellfish on the hard ground. The gulls then swoop down and pull the contents out of the broken shells.

Three varieties of herons feed in the marsh: the short green heron, the great blue heron, and the black-crowned night heron. You may also spot marsh hawks, egrets, and short-eared owls.

These birds are drawn to the salt marsh to feed on fish and

23. Wasque Reservation

The two-hundred-acre Wasque Reservation, located at the southeastern tip of Chappaquiddick Island, is surrounded by water on three sides. Miles of secluded sandy barrier beach separate Wasque's southern tip from the Atlantic Ocean's dynamic surf. On the west side lies calm Katama Bay, a haven for windsurfers and clammers. Poucha Pond and Muskeget Channel bound Wasque on the east.

Once you reach Wasque (pronounced Way-skwee) and look west toward Edgartown, you'll discover that Chappaquiddick is not really an island but a peninsula. Chappaquiddick has truly been an island only ten times in the last two hundred years, when violent storms created a breach in the barrier beach connecting Chappaquiddick and Edgartown. Whenever that happened, no vehicles could travel the three-mile stretch from Edgartown South Beach to Wasque Point, the premier bluefishing spot on Martha's Vineyard.

Wasque has a lot more going for it besides its ability to draw striped bass and bluefish. It possesses an endless sandy beach with waves to daunt even the most intrepid bodysurfer. A property of the Trustees of Reservations, Wasque Reservation offers hiking, swimming, and picnicking in a protected, unspoiled environment.

DIRECTIONS: *From the ferry, follow the paved road for 3.8 miles, until it becomes a dirt road. Continue on the dirt road for 1.2 miles. You can bike to Wasque, but you will have to navigate an unpaved, sandy road. If you have a mountain or hybrid bike or are prepared to walk the sandy sections, you can avoid the possibility of facing a filled-*

Dusty miller

Seaside goldenrod

protected side of the dune hosts a variety of plants. Look for the delicate blue-gray **dusty miller**, which produces small yellow flowers in the summer. Its fuzzy, dusty-looking protective covering helps the plant conserve water so that it can grow in arid conditions. You may also spot **seaside goldenrod**, another plant that has adapted to this harsh environment. In the fall it decorates the sand with its clusters of bright yellow flowers.

Upon reaching the beach, you are faced with a decision: to swim, sun, sleep, or stroll. If your choice is swimming, either turn left toward the calmer waters of East Beach or right toward Katama Bay. Avoid Wasque Point, which lies at the end of the fishermen's boardwalk and is usually crowded with fishermen and their four-wheel-drive vehicles. Fish abound at Wasque Point because of the convergence of currents flowing toward the east and south. Because of the strong undertow here, swimming in this section of beach is not recommended.

If you turn right at Wasque Point, you'll be strolling on the two-mile-long barrier beach that separates the ocean and Katama Bay. This section of sand is a good example of up-island loss becoming down-island gain. Although erosion annually sweeps away about eight feet of the Vineyard's southern shoreline, strong easterly currents have carried the sand from up-island cliffs and beaches to create this barrier beach.

You may spot sandpipers, small birds with long bills, which prefer isolated beaches where they peacefully can chase each receding wave in their quest for sand fleas. The sand fleas, or

24. Oak Bluffs Camp Ground

Oak Bluffs, the first Vineyard town to become a summer resort, continues to have a lively resort atmosphere. Its compact harbor welcomes boats filled with tourists interested in having a good time, and the town itself obliges. It offers nightclubs, fast-food spots, video-game stores, and one of the oldest platform carousels in the country.

But Oak Bluffs is much more than escape and entertainment. Although settled later than other island towns, it has its own distinctive history, centered on its origins as the Methodist Camp Meeting Place, a section of town now known as the Camp Ground. Exploring this area, which is filled with quaint Victorian homes adorned with brightly colored gingerbread trim, is a must for every Vineyard visitor.

Walking Time: Varies, but you should allow at least 1 hour

Begin where New York Avenue meets Oak Bluffs Harbor. As you travel down New York Avenue, past the harbor on your left, you will see Sunset Lake on the right.

Originally, Sunset Lake and Oak Bluffs Harbor were one body of water, which was called Squash Meadow Pond. But the dredging of the harbor and of the channel into Vineyard Sound separated the two. The building of the causeway between the pond and the harbor further defined the separation.

The Wesley Hotel, on Lake Avenue across from the harbor, is an example of the grand wooden hotels, with their large and inviting verandas, that were popular a hundred years ago. Unfortunately, these structures frequently burned down.

Although a fire did once destroy the Wesley, it was rebuilt and today is the sole survivor of the Victorian-era hotels.

Continue past the Wesley Hotel, toward the business district, until you reach a major intersection with an Information Booth perched in the middle. If you arrive by bike, you can park your cycle in the bike rack that is on the right side, next to the Island Theater. Stay to the right and head up Circuit Avenue, walking past all the shops and restaurants, until you reach a tiny side street named Tabernacle Avenue. You'll see a sign announcing the entrance to the **Martha's Vineyard Camp Meeting Grounds**. Turn right.

An interesting speculation is whether Martha's Vineyard would have developed as a resort island if Oak Bluffs had not become a popular site for religious meetings. It is hard to believe that an island this beautiful, so close to the populous cities of the East Coast, would have remained a farming and fishing community forever. But it took the religious fervor of the island's summer visitors to jump-start the habit of annual pilgrimages to the Vineyard.

In the early nineteenth century, a resurgence of religion gave birth to the annual summer gatherings. Proponents of the Methodist movement were vigorously seeking converts. These preachers had found that outdoor camp meetings, with their emotional expressions of faith, were well-suited for proseltyzing. In search of a new meeting place, Jeremiah Pease of Edgartown looked for a remote undeveloped area near the seashore. He found, near Squash Meadow Pond, a secluded spot shaded by a large grove of oak trees. In the summer of 1835, the Methodists pitched their tents and established the Martha's Vineyard Camp Meeting. They called the area Wesleyan Grove.

For many summers church groups from Providence, New Bedford, Boston, and Nantucket attended the meetings under the oak trees. Worshipers sat on rough benches and slept in small tents that were interspersed among the tall trees. As the number of families grew, the tents became larger. Some congregations constructed huge tents, which they partitioned down the middle to separate the sexes.

The congregants found their annual meetings so pleasurable

To individualize his cottage, an owner often would cover it with filigree and add his own special decoration. Number 14 has a unique pointed gazebo, while other residences have distinctive color combinations.

A house (4) with a radically different design can be found on the far right corner of Pawtucket Avenue. It is built of one-piece pine boards that start at the ground floor and travel up to the third story.

Another unusual sight (5) is on the corner of Fourth Avenue: a lot with flowers, bushes, and trees, but no cottages. Three homes once stood on this land, but all were bought by the resident living to the left, who gardens this plot.

Although the owners have purchased their cottages, the land is owned by the Martha's Vineyard Camp Meeting Grounds Association, which issues annual leases to the purchasers. The Association directors have the option of not renewing the leases of undesirable tenants.

Continue to walk around the Camp Ground and look at these colorful dwellings, representative of Carpenter Gothic architecture. These homes are literally spotlighted during Illumination Night, which usually occurs during the third week in August (the date varies and is not advertised until the last minute, in order to keep down the crowds). Each cottage, illuminated by ornate and colorful Japanese-style lanterns, tries to outdo its neighbors in the number and variety of its lights. Throngs of viewers parade by on the sidewalks, while the cottage owners and their friends party on front porches and gaze at the spectators strolling by.

Illumination Night began in 1869 as an annual celebration of the closing of the religious meetings. The recent addition of a singalong band concert has made this unique event even more festive.

After walking around the Camp Ground, return to Tabernacle Avenue and proceed out to Circuit Avenue, a good place to stop for food or drink. Mad Martha's makes the best ice cream on the planet; Cozy's creates sandwiches and also sells ice cream. Subway sells great grinders and Giordano's, at 107 Circuit Avenue across from the Information Booth, prepares delicious pizza that you can eat in the restaurant or take out.

25. Tisbury Meadow, Wompesket, and Ripley's Field Preserves

Here are three interconnected nature preserves that you can explore either on bike or on foot.

The Martha's Vineyard Land Bank, a conservation organization, has cut trails through these three properties and connected them. A hiker can choose to hike one, two, or three of the preserves.

All three properties are ideal destinations for birders. Each has meadows that attract a wide variety of birds, including mockingbirds, tree swallows, chipping sparrows, northern orioles, and prairie warblers.

During the summer, an array of wildflowers dot the fields, adding a colorful contrast to the shrubs and grasses.

In Tisbury Meadow and Ripley's Field, the trails are wide and make for enjoyable off-road biking. Your big decision is which mode of transportation to choose in order to best explore the varied terrain. Hiking the three areas takes about three hours while biking takes less than half that time.

Tisbury Meadow and Ripley's Field are larger properties, 83 and 56 acres respectively, and have similar terrain: meadows leading to hilly wooded areas. Although Wompesket is the smallest area, encompassing only 18 acres, its landscape is more diverse, consisting of wetlands, ponds, woods, and a large meadow. Tisbury Meadow and Ripley's Field can be accessed directly from main roads but Wompesket requires hiking or biking on an ancient road and access trail for a mile before reaching the preserve. The distance between each of the areas is approximately a mile.

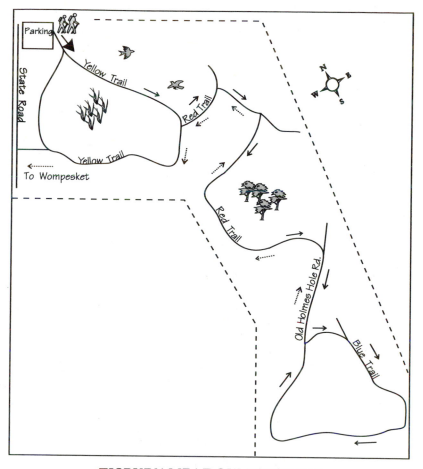

TISBURY MEADOW PRESERVE

The Red Trail travels through typical Vineyard forest consisting of tall, stately oak trees hovering over huckleberry and blueberry bushes. When the trail forks, bear right.

At the second fork, look for the Red Trail marker and bear right. The trail climbs up and down, the result of glacial action that took place thousands of years ago. The felled trees scattered throughout the forest were victims of Hurricane Bob, which blasted the Vineyard in August 1991.

monarch butterfly, which feeds on its small blooms. Native Americans called this plant pleurisy root, because they believed that chewing on its tough stem would cure them of pleurisy, a lung disease that plagued early settlers.

As you approach the road, the trail forks. If you bear right, you'll return to the parking lot. If you proceed straight, you'll reach State Road. Almost directly across State Road is a small dirt road. A left off this road and through the stone barricade leads to Red Coat Hill Road. There, you'll find a wetland marker directing you on toward Wompesket Preserve.

FROM TISBURY MEADOW PRESERVE TO WOMPESKET PRESERVE

Red Coat Hill Road is another one of the Vineyard's "ancient ways." If you look at the road in relation to the terrain on either side, you'll notice how much lower the road is, evidence of generations of Vineyarders traveling this route. Hundreds of years ago, when the Vineyard consisted mainly of farmland, the view from the highest point on this road included a clear shot of Vineyard Haven Harbor. This lookout was vital to the island's defense against the threat of British invasion during the Revolutionary War. However, in September 1778 General Sir Charles Grey led his British brigadiers up this road and seized the high ground. The road's name is a reminder of this historic event.

Remain on Red Coat Hill Road and cross two intersections with other unpaved roads. The first intersection is Shubael Weeks Road, which leads to Ripley's Field Preserve. At the intersection with Merry Farm Road, the first paved road, turn right. Follow the road up toward the farm.

Just before the road forks, look to your right for another wetlands marker. Follow the trail that skirts the edge of Merry Farm. Look to your left at the unusually shaped oak tree standing alone in the meadow. Its misshapen limbs result from the continual gusts of salt-laden winds.

Beyond the tree is a view of the island's south shore and the Atlantic Ocean.

* * *

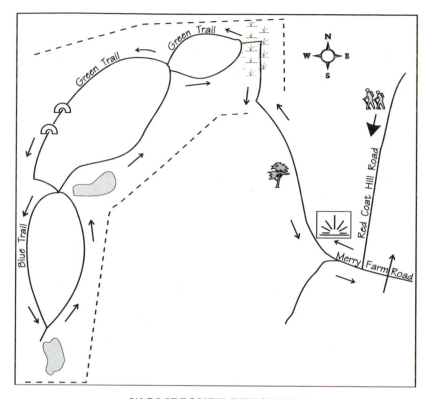

WOMPESKET PRESERVE

thick-stemmed, dark green leaves, leathery and shiny, that when crushed give off the familiar bayberry scent.

Walk through the meadow until you reach a small pond and the end of the trail. If you're lucky enough to be hiking in August, when the blackberries are in season, stop and snack.

Reverse direction and fork right to return on the opposite side of the meadow. You'll find many Russian olive trees growing here. An introduced species, this shrub, with its long, slender leaves with silvery undersurfaces, has proliferated on the island.

While strolling through the meadow, you'll observe an unusual growth pattern: several chokecherry trees with multiple stems. Look for the tree that has 16 separate stems growing from

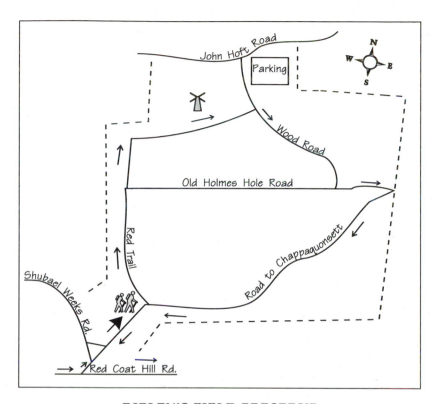

RIPLEY'S FIELD PRESERVE

A previous owner used the wind's energy to pull water from the pond for use in irrigation. However, the windmill broke and, instead of replacing it, the owner allowed the pond to dry up. From the meadow, the trail reenters the woodland filled with tall pine and oak trees.

At the "T" intersection, turn right. (A left turn leads to the preserve parking area.)

Bear left at the fork.

Turn right onto the Road to Chappaquonsett.

Continue to bend left until you reach Shubael Weeks Road, where you turn left.

Follow Shubael Weeks Road until it intersects with Red Coat Hill Road. Turn left and return to State Road.

Cottonwood

Woods, and follow the trail into the woods. The hike in the woods will take about fifteen minutes.

While on the trail watch for two varieties of trees not commonly found on the island. The pignut hickory has pointed, fine-toothed leaflets and bears round, hard-shelled nuts. These nuts grow in husks that split into four parts when broken. **Cottonwood** trees, with their shiny, green, triangular leaves, also grow in these woods. In the spring, their small green flowers droop in long clusters called catkins. The flowers eventually become masses of cottony seeds.

Remnants of earlier generations can be found in these woods. As you walk, keep your eyes open for an old root cellar, along with other excavations that were the basements of sheep farmers' homes two hundred years ago. The settlers had clear-cut this land, using the trees for fuel and shelter. The uneven and crumbling stone walls fenced in the sheep that grazed on these pastures. This land reverted back to woods when farming ceased being profitable.

27. Cedar Tree Neck
Wildlife Sanctuary

Cedar Tree Neck Wildlife Sanctuary consists of three hundred acres of varied terrain. Three trails—leading to beaches, bluffs, streams, freshwater ponds, woods, and a sphagnum bog—provide a broad sample of the Vineyard's ecosystems. Panoramic views to the north include Vineyard Sound and all of the Elizabeth Islands. Tranquil hiking in this remote sanctuary provides a relaxing exploration of diverse flora and fauna.

DIRECTIONS: *Traveling west on State Road in West Tisbury, turn right on Indian Hill Road. Follow this road for 1.3 miles. At Obed Daggett Road, turn right. Look for signs for the sanctuary, and follow them for 1 mile.*

Hiking Time: 2 hours

Cedar Tree Neck Wildlife Sanctuary was acquired through a cooperative fundraising campaign by the Sheriff's Meadow Foundation, a land conservation organization, and the Massachusetts Audubon Society. The Sheriff's Meadow Foundation aims to protect natural areas as living museums; neither swimming nor picnicking is allowed in any of their properties.

This hike can be as long or as short as you wish. There are three separate trails—White, Red, and Yellow—each with many special features. Walking all the trails will take about two hours and is well worth the time and energy.

Begin by going to the left on the White Trail, which starts to the side of the parking lot. At the beginning of this trail are two collected. Since water cannot flow out of this low-lying area and there are no underground streams to provide additional water, it just sits there. The production of oxygen, which is necessary for decaying and composting to occur, requires the movement of water. Sphagnum moss can grow in boggy areas where there is little oxygen. The sphagnum serves as a cleansing mechanism, secreting acids that inhibit bacterial action. Since organisms that die in the bog decay very slowly due to the lack of oxygen, a bog is a good resource for scientists to discover what was living in this region thousands of years ago. Sphagnum moss is also useful in gardens for keeping soil loose and retaining moisture.

Look around and notice what types of plants are growing near the bog. The swamp azalea's sweet-smelling flower, white and vase-shaped, blooms in July and August. The sweet pepperbush, with its small, fragrant, white flowers clustered in short spikes, is another shrub that grows in swampy areas.

The White Trail circles around, eventually reaching the beach, from which you can see Vineyard Sound and the Elizabeth Islands. Naushon, the island directly ahead, is the largest of the chain. To the far left lies Cuttyhunk, which contains the town of Gosnold, the governmental center of the Elizabeth Islands. The other islands are privately owned.

After strolling on the beach, shelling, or just relaxing and enjoying the ocean, you can resume your hike by turning right along the beach. Continue past the boardwalk and one Red Trail marker and walk alongside the fence that prevents people from walking on the dunes. The fence stops at the beginning of the trail, indicated by a second Red Trail marker, that leads to the bluff.

At the fork, head to the left through a section of typical beach vegetation, including *Rosa rugosa*, bayberry, and pasture rose. During your climb, step into the cleared lookouts for panoramic views of the Elizabeth Islands, Buzzards Bay, and Woods Hole.

As the trail veers inland, the vegetation changes and you will find yourself under a canopy formed by the arching branches of sassafras and tupelo trees.

Descend from the bluff and return to the beach. Walk back along the fence to the continuation of the Red Trail at the next marker indicates the spot where two streams join. The larger stream then empties into Cedar Tree Neck Pond, from which the water travels underground into the ocean.

After the second stream crossing, bear left at the fork. As you walk, look up to your right for Cedar Tree Neck's famous bonsai (or pygmy) beech trees. These hundred-year-old trees would normally have grown to a height of eighty feet, but because they are on a ridge overlooking the ocean and are regularly blasted by the salt-laden wind, they are quite small. Their wide trunks attest to their age, but their angular horizontal branches have been shaped by fierce wintery gales.

Retrace your steps and follow the left fork of the Yellow Trail back to the parking lot.

28. Long Point Wildlife Refuge

Visitors love Long Point because of its magnificent secluded beach. One reason Long Point remains relatively uncrowded is its remote location at the end of a seemingly endless bumpy, sandy road. But the main reason for its unpopulated beach is the refuge's small parking lot, which is often filled by 11 A.M. However, cyclists are never refused entry. They also avoid paying the $6 automobile charge, although they do have to pay the $3 adult entry fee. Children under 15 are admitted free.

On a great beach day, this 633-acre reservation is worth the hassle. You can jump the waves in the ocean, or stroll over to the calm waters of Long Cove Pond to swim and sun in a more protected environment. You can walk for miles along the coast or head inland and explore the refuge on the hiking trails that skirt the edges of the pond and cove.

DIRECTIONS: *The summer entrance, open 10 to 6 daily from June 15 to September 15, is located off the south side of the Edgartown–West Tisbury Road, 0.3 miles west of the airport entrance. If you're traveling west from Edgartown, it's the second dirt road on the left after the airport. The off-season entrance, via Deep Bottom Road, is 0.8 miles further west.*

Hiking time: 1 hour on trails; unlimited beach walking

The Trustees of Reservations, the oldest land trust in the world, owns and maintains Long Point. Three other Trustees properties are described in this book: Menemsha Hills Reservation in Chilmark (see Chapter 32), and Wasque

Beach pea   *Beach grass*

conserves moisture in its long blades by curling inward to avoid the sun's drying rays.

The summer access to the refuge and beach travels between Long Cove Pond on the right and Big Homer's Pond on the left. The numerous small ponds and coves on the southern side of the island were originally created by streams from melting glacial ice. After the glacier disappeared, the streams dried up, leaving wide openings which then filled with a combination of sea water and fresh water from underground springs. These coves and ponds continue to be a mix of fresh and salt water.

The beach is typical of the Vineyard's south coast beaches: sandy with heavy surf. The bathers on the left side are typically West Tisbury residents, who are issued a permit to use this beach. As you walk to the right, you'll find fewer and fewer bathers.

In order to further explore Long Point Wildlife Refuge, turn right and walk past Long Cove Pond until you reach the next beach entrance. Follow this path, the Orange Trail, through the sandplain grassland, with Long Cove Pond on your right. Make sure that you remain on authorized trails so as to not disturb the resident wildlife.

The path forks. Leave the Orange Trail and bear right onto the Yellow Trail. This path meanders through an oak woodland with

29. Sepiessa Point Reservation

Sepiessa Point Reservation is notable for its scenic beauty and for its access to Tisbury Great Pond. You can hike, picnic, and swim at Sepiessa Point, or you can launch your sailboat or canoe at the reservation's landing.

At 164 acres, this is the largest property of the Martha's Vineyard Land Bank Commission. The Land Bank, a conservation organization, appropriates a 2% tax on real-estate transfers and uses the funds to purchase land. If the property lends itself to recreational use, the Land Bank develops trails and invites the public to explore the terrain. One of the main reasons for the purchase of Sepiessa Point was to allow public access to Tisbury Great Pond.

DIRECTIONS: *Travel west on the Edgartown–West Tisbury Road into West Tisbury. Turn left onto New Lane, which becomes Tiah's Cove Road, and travel 1.2 miles. The reservation is on the right.*

Hiking time: 70 minutes

The hike begins on an old road that follows the shore of Tiah's Cove. The road passes by the boat launching area, marked by a red flag. Soon after, you'll notice a trail marker on the path on the left side of the road.

Turn left onto the trail that winds through a pitch pine forest, and then a woodland of scrub oak trees and huckleberry bushes.

The path heads toward Tississa Pond. The clearings near the pond allow a clear view of the farm on the other side. A fence extends into the water to prevent the farm's goats from drowning. Watch for the eagle-like osprey that may be perching on the pole at the southern tip of the farm or plunging feet first into the water in search of fish.

As you hike, keep a look out for the rare northern harrier, a marsh hawk around two feet long that often glides close to the ground searching for prey. The males are pale gray and the females are brown.

As you walk closer to Tisbury Great Pond, the trees become smaller and the vegetation sparser due to the wind and salt spray. Growing in this sunny sandplain section are plants that are usually not found on the mainland, such as sandplain flax, Nantucket shadbush, and bushy rockrose. The caribou moss growing along the trail is further evidence of the harsh climatic conditions in this area.

From the shore of Tisbury Great Pond, look south directly across the water to the barrier beach and the Atlantic Ocean. To the left lies Long Point, the Trustees of Reservations property that is explored in Chapter 28.

As you walk along the beach, try to locate several of the ten coves and ponds that extend out from Tisbury Great Pond like fingers on a hand, with Black Point Pond forming the thumb.

The oyster shells scattered on the sand are the result of oyster seeding in the pond. Since oysters require salt water to breed, twice a year a breach is created in the barrier beach to allow the ocean to flow through to the pond.

Blue-claw crabs also inhabit Tisbury Great Pond. During low tide people armed with nets wade in the water and attempt to scoop up the fast-moving crabs. The shells of both crabs and oysters create a hazard for unshod swimmers.

The return trip through the reservation travels along the same trail. Hidden in the woods is the weather-beaten shack that housed the former owner of this land.

When the trail meets the road, turn right to return to the parking lot.

30. Mill Brook Woods Preserve and Waskosim's Rock Reservation

This hike takes you through a diversity of terrains, each with a rich variety of flora and fauna. You can follow a brook as it weaves through a woodland and you can climb to the top of one of Martha's Vineyard's highest peaks. There you can admire the mammoth Waskosim's Rock, situated on a sacred Wampanoag site. The Martha's Vineyard Land Bank Commission, which owns and maintains Waskosim's Rock Reservation, permits biking on its well-maintained trails.

DIRECTIONS: *The reservation is located off the south side of North Road, about a mile and a half west of the junction with State Road and soon after the West Tisbury–Chilmark town line. The Land Bank logo sign indicates the entrance to Mill Brook Woods Preserve, which leads to Waskosim's Rock Reservation. A bike rack is located in the parking lot.*

Hiking time: 2 hours

Waskosim's Rock dominates one of the highest points on Martha's Vineyard. The mammoth stone, which dwarfs all the surrounding rocks, was dumped here by a receding glacier. The rock's original silhouette was altered by a bolt of lightning that created a fissure down the center large enough to conceal two or three people. Rumor has it that Waskosim's Rock was once a favorite hideaway for fugitives.

The Indian chiefs Nashawakemmuck and Takemmy probably gave the rock its name. They are said to have used Waskosim's Rock as a boundary between their properties. Matthew Mayhew, a Vineyard settler, continued this tradition, with the rock

Virginia creeper

Continue further on the Red Trail. Look out to your right for a view of the Vineyard Sound foothills, including Mill Brook and its surrounding valley. This deep, narrow valley was known for generations as Zephaniah's Holler, named after Captain Zephaniah Mayhew, one of the early settlers on Martha's Vineyard.

Many years ago, when the Vineyard consisted mainly of farmland and was not so densely forested, Waskosim's Rock was observable from a great distance and was a popular visiting place. Farmers and their families would climb to the site to picnic and enjoy the view.

Continue on the Red Trail through a meadow that is frequently filled with birds, including doves, bobwhites, starlings, robins, swallows, goldfinches, crows, and hawks. The stone wall, one of many on the island, once served as a boundary for the cows and sheep that grazed on this land. The abandoned foundation that sits in the meadow belonged to the Allen family, who farmed the land a hundred years ago.

In the field you'll see the hyssop-leaved thoroughwort, also known as boneset, with its fuzzy white clusters of small flowers that bloom in late summer and fall. (It's called "boneset" for its traditional use in folk healing.) Queen Anne's lace blooms through the summer, displaying flat-topped clusters of tiny

31. Fulling Mill Brook Preserve and Middle Road Sanctuary

One of my favorite picnic spots on the Vineyard is the boulder-lined bank of Fulling Mill Brook. Nearly a mile of the brook flows through the Fulling Mill Brook Preserve, located between Middle Road and South Road in Chilmark.

A hiker who lunches in the preserve can take a half-mile walk up the road to Middle Road Sanctuary to dessert on the blueberry and huckleberry bushes scattered throughout that property. The sanctuary, administered by the Sheriff's Meadow Foundation, has trails that wind through woodlands and ascend to one of the island's highest peaks, overlooking the south coast and Chilmark Pond. Exploring these two areas provides an hour and a half of enjoyable up-island hiking.

DIRECTIONS: *As you travel west along Middle Road, the entrance to Fulling Mill Brook Preserve is on the left, a half mile beyond the intersection with Tabor House Road.*

Hiking time: 90 minutes, for both properties

FULLING MILL BROOK PRESERVE

This 46-acre preserve is owned jointly by the town of Chilmark and the Martha's Vineyard Land Bank. Within its boundaries is Fulling Mill Brook, one of the best trout streams on the island. The mill was formerly located at the South Road entrance, near the lower and faster-flowing section of the brook. As you go down the gravel road into the preserve, *look carefully* on the right for a small hiking-trail sign next to a dirt path. Turn right onto the path.

river make perfect picnic tables. Do not drink the water, which is likely to be full of bacteria. Do carry out your trash.

Return to the main path and turn right to continue your exploration. After walking for five minutes, you'll reach South Road. There you'll see another entrance to the preserve—an imposing one with stone columns and walls.

To return, retrace your steps. In about twenty minutes you will be back at the Middle Road entrance.

FROM FULLING MILL BROOK PRESERVE TO MIDDLE ROAD SANCTUARY

At the gravel road, turn left to reach Middle Road.

Turn right onto Middle Road. Travel past Tabor House Road and the old entrance to Middle Road Sanctuary. The new entrance to Middle Road Sanctuary follows immediately on the right.

MIDDLE ROAD SANCTUARY

Over the past 35 years the Sheriff's Meadow Foundation has acquired or received more than 1,700 acres of land on Martha's Vineyard. Some of these properties are protected land and are not open to the public. Others, like Middle Road Sanctuary, provide visitors with the opportunity for a relaxing hike through varied island terrain. The name "sanctuary" describes how the foundation wants its properties to be used: communing with nature is fine, but neither biking, picnicking, nor camping is allowed. However, there are no rules prohibiting picking the succulent huckleberries and blueberries that grow throughout this 90-acre sanctuary.

Many varieties of birds are spotted in this area, including great-crested flycatchers, downy and hairy woodpeckers, red-tailed hawks, Carolina wrens, and chickadees.

Begin this 2.6-mile hike by walking along the trail until you reach a fork. Bear right onto the beginning of the Red Trail. This trail loops around through a common variety of Vineyard

formerly served as a boundary between the sheep farms that occupied this land.

The path meets an unpaved road. Cross the road and look directly ahead for the Yellow Trail marker. Continue on the path, passing a house on the right. The gnarled branches of the low scrub oak trees result from the winds that batter this peak. Soon you will come to a short path on the left, where a glacial erratic sits under a black oak tree. From behind the erratic you can look out over Chilmark Pond and the Atlantic Ocean.

The trail meanders through a heavily wooded section until it ends at an ancient dirt road named the King's Highway. If you turn left and follow this for almost a half mile, you'll reach another old unpaved way, named Meetinghouse Road. Another left turn and 0.7 miles more will bring you back to Middle Road.

If you are returning via the same route, follow the Yellow Trail until it merges with the Red Trail. Turn right onto the Red Trail to hike the remaining one-third mile to the entrance. Again, you'll hike through an oak woodland with huckleberry bushes covering the ground. Another large glacial erratic appears on the left.

32. Menemsha and Menemsha Hills Reservation

"**M**enemsha," translated from the Wampanoag language, means "place of observation"—a fitting description of this picturesque village, which is, indeed, a great place to look around. Located within the greater town of Chilmark, Menemsha is bounded by Menemsha Pond, Menemsha Basin, and Vineyard Sound. A walk along the town's long dock takes the observer along Menemsha Basin, past fishing shanties, lobster boats, and colorful buoys to Menemsha Bight, where pleasure craft sail into and out of Menemsha Pond. Nearby is Menemsha's compact public beach, which draws bathers who favor its calm waters.

A hike through Menemsha Hills Reservation, a 211-acre Trustees of Reservations property, includes a climb to the top of Prospect Hill for sweeping views of both the north and south coasts, and then a walk to the beach where you can swim, sun, or stroll.

DIRECTIONS: *To reach Menemsha, go west on North Road until it ends. Menemsha Hills Reservation is on the north side of North Road, one mile east of Mememsha.*

Hiking times:
  Menemsha: 30 minutes
  Menemsha Hills Reservation: 90 minutes

MENEMSHA

After your arrival into the village, continue down the road toward the water, passing the Home Port Restaurant, which including the 308-foot-high Prospect Hill, one of the Vineyard's highest points, has made the reservation into a quite desirable destination.

On a hot summer day, this hike can be taxing. Don't forget to bring a water bottle.

The trail head is behind the trail map on the north side of the parking lot. Follow the path to a fork in the trail, and bear left for the half-mile ascent to Prospect Hill. If you are hiking this trail during midsummer, you will be able to feast on the blueberries growing on the bushes that line the trail. Tall viburnum bushes display their large white flowers in July.

At the next fork, bear left to the peak. Later, you will return down this path in order to head toward the beach.

The top of Prospect Hill marks the furthest reach of the last glacier that moved southward from the Hudson Bay area around twenty thousand years ago. During its slow journey, the glacier collected much of the surface landscape; when it melted, it deposited its accumulation of stones, boulders, clay, and other debris. The hillier, rockier sections of the Vineyard, such as Prospect Hill, are called the moraine.

From the peak, the view to the north includes Vineyard Sound, the Elizabeth Islands, Buzzards Bay, and the Massachusetts coast. To the west you see Menemsha and its harbor, Menemsha Pond, Squibnocket Pond, Lobsterville Beach, and Gay Head. To the south lies the Atlantic Ocean.

Retrace your steps until you return to the fork. Now turn left onto the mile-long trail that leads to the Great Sand Cliffs. The path travels through a brushy section, crosses a dirt road, and then weaves through an area whose topography is quite different from Prospect Hill.

This section is filled with unusual oak trees with long branches that extend out rather than up. In their early growing period, these trees probably were decapitated, after which they resprouted. Whether sheep grazed on the young oaks or the trees were repeatedly cut down, the results were the same: the determined saplings sent out new shoots and grew additional stems. With no other trees around to crowd them, the oaks

33. Gay Head Cliffs and Beach

Gay Head lures busloads of visitors who come to see its spectacular cliffs and beach. But the town itself is interesting because it has maintained its Native American heritage. Gay Head is one of two Indian townships in Massachusetts. Although most of the Wampanoags no longer earn their livings farming and fishing as their ancestors did, many have remained in this tiny, remote town and have become proprietors of the shops that straddle the cliffs.

On a clear day, the panorama from the viewing area on top of the 150-foot cliffs is the most spectacular on the island. After you have climbed to the top, you must descend to sea level for another not-to-be-missed attraction: a walk on the beach alongside the cliffs.

Strolling along the Gay Head beach is as pleasurable as gazing down from above. The majestic cliffs rise steeply out of the sand to flaunt their colorful striations. A wide, sandy beach, dotted with a variety of rocks, follows the cliffs around the western tip of the island. The beachgoers, in bathing and birthday suits, prance in and out of the water and often wallow—illegally—in the clay pits. Then they amble along the beach, covered only with the clay residue from the pits.

DIRECTIONS: *Travel west on South Road through the town of Gay Head. The cliffs are at the end of the road.*

Hiking time: Unlimited beach hiking

cook fish and shellfish on the sand. This is the likely origin of the seaside clambake.

After snacking and shopping on the cliffs, you can walk on the boardwalk down to the beach. If you are biking, you can mount and ride down to the beach entrance, off of Moshup's Trail. There is a bike rack on the sand after you enter the beach. To access Moshup's Trail, turn right after you leave the parking area at the cliffs.

GAY HEAD BEACH

Be prepared for a ten-minute hike from the parking lot down to the beach. Upon reaching the beach, go for a swim if you'd like, and then begin your stroll around the tip of the island.

This hike is as good as beach walking gets. Because the beach curves around the island, the vista out into the ocean continually changes. The cliffs, the only constant, loom over the beach, providing a multicolored presence at your side. Their colors vary depending on the location and the time of day, from midday tones of amber and slate to warm reds and oranges at sunset.

The beach's southern side exhibits an assortment of rocks scattered by the frequent storms that have battered this shore. The beach tends to be sandier on this side and families settle here to swim and picnic. Once you round the bend and head up the rockier northern coast, you'll notice changes in both the beach and its occupants. Because this section is more remote, it attracts couples who wish to sun and swim unencumbered by bathing suits. Some wallow in the clay at the foot of the cliffs and emerge coated with the dirt. However, environmentalists are rightfully concerned about the clay bathing, since it accelerates the already rapid erosion of the cliffs. Now the clay baths are illegal and anyone caught partaking of that pleasure pays a hefty fine.

Once you reach the tip, look out, directly ahead, into the ocean for the small, uninhabited Noman's Land Island. The island was not always deserted. In the nineteenth century, Vineyard fishermen spent at least six months a year there,

Appendix

Emergency

Police, Fire, Ambulance, 911

Martha's Vineyard Hospital, Linton Lane, Oak Bluffs, 693-0410

Bicycle Shops

VINEYARD HAVEN

Cycle Works, 105 State Road, 693-6966. Rentals, sales, repairs.

Martha's Bicycle Rental, 4 Lagoon Pond Road, 693-6593. Rentals, sales, repairs.

Martha's Vineyard Scooter and Bike, Union Street, 693-0782. Rentals, sales, repairs.

OAK BLUFFS

Anderson Bike Rentals, Circuit Avenue Extension, 693-9346. Rentals, sales, repairs.

DeBettencourt's Bike Shop, Circuit Avenue Extension, 693-0011. Rentals.

King's Rental, Circuit Avenue Extension, 693-1887. Rentals, sales.

Ride-On Mopeds and Bikes, Circuit Avenue Extension, 693-2076. Rentals, sales, repairs.

Sun-N-Fun, Lake Avenue, 693-5457. Rentals, sales, repairs.

EDGARTOWN

Be Wheel Happy, 8 South Water Street, 627-5928. Rentals.

R. W. Cutler, Main Street, 627-4052; Triangle, 627-7099. Rentals, sales, repairs.

Edgartown Bicycles, 190 Upper Main Street, 627-9008. Rentals, sales, repairs.

Pharmacies

VINEYARD HAVEN

Leslie's Drug Store, Main Street, 693-1010

OAK BLUFFS

Oak Bluffs Pharmacy, 142 Circuit Avenue, 693-4501

EDGARTOWN

Triangle Pharmacy, 245 Vineyard Haven Road, 627-5107

WEST TISBURY

Conroy Apothecary, State Road, 693-7070

Service stations

VINEYARD HAVEN

Seward Enterprises, 40 Beach Road, 693-5060

Vineyard Service Station, 7–9 Beach Road, 696-7383

OAK BLUFFS

N. J. DeBettencourt and Sons, New York Avenue, 693-0751

EDGARTOWN

Edgartown Texaco, 199 Upper Main Street, 627-4715

WEST TISBURY

Up-Island Automotive, State Road, 693-5166

CHILMARK

Menemsha Texaco Service, Basin Road, 645-2641

Automobile Parking Areas for Bikers

VINEYARD HAVEN

Tisbury School, between Spring and William Streets.

OAK BLUFFS

Martha's Vineyard Regional High School, Edgartown–Vineyard
Haven Road.

EDGARTOWN

Trolley shuttle lot, on Dark Woods Road off the
Edgartown–Vineyard Haven Road, east of the Triangle
Shopping Area.

Trolley shuttle lot, on Robinson Road between Pease's Point Way
and the Edgartown–West Tisbury Road.

Index of Destinations